250

DEDICATED **SUPPLEMENTS** FOR **DEDICATED** sports people

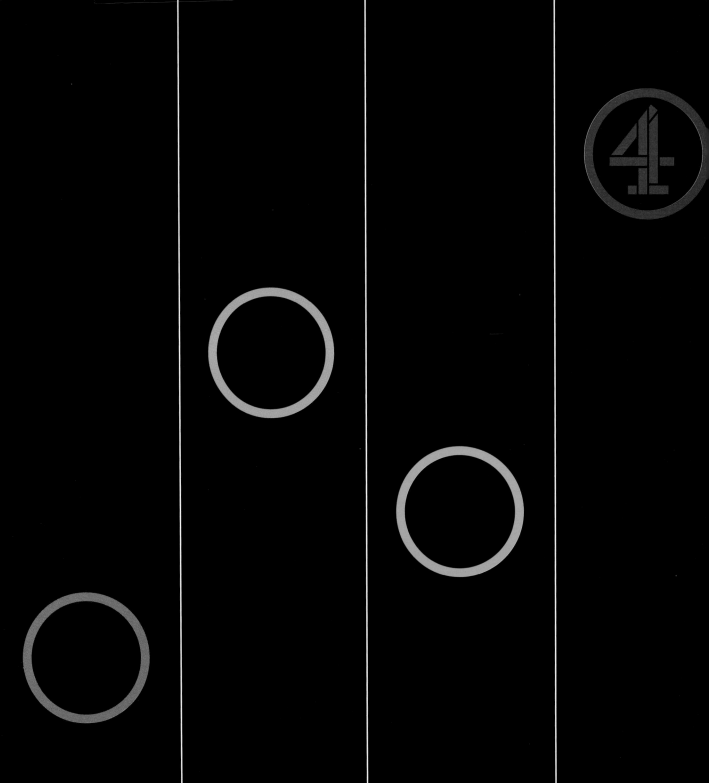

FIRST OFF THE BLOCKS. NOW ON YOUR BOX

BRITISH ATHLETIC FEDERATION

British
ATHLETICS
Yearbook 1997

Editor
Duncan Mackay

KOGAN
PAGE

BEHIND
EACH AND EVERY ATHLET

FOR WHATEVER SHOULD LIE

AHEAD

WORKING HAND IN HAND.
REEBOK AND THE BRITISH ATHLETICS FEDERATION.

British Athletics

A COMPREHENSIVE APPROACH

Behind Weleda's comprehensive range of natural medicines there lies an important philosophy concerning the way in which we take care of our health, and how we should relate to the world around us. The pursuit of health without exploitation is one of the central values of Weleda. There is nothing new about the company's principles - they have been maintained since 1921 when Weleda was founded. It isn't a marketing ploy - it's a whole way of life.

Weleda endorses a very individual approach to healthcare, aiming to treat the whole person rather than just the symptoms of illness, by stimulating the natural healing process within each of us. It's an approach that echoes the thinking of Samuel Hahnemann over 200 years ago when he established the principles of homoeopathy, and it is not surprising that today Weleda produces a wide range of homoeopathic remedies.

In the 1920s through the work of Dr Rudolf Steiner and Dr Ita Wegman, in combination with Hahnemann's ideas, Weleda developed a wide selection of anthroposophic medicines. The result is an extensive homoeopathically-prepared range that takes into account the full nature of man.

Over the past 70 years Weleda has also developed a cruelty-free bodycare range made from natural plant ingredients to produce skincare, haircare, babycare and dentalcare products. Only the best raw materials are used, and every single ingredient is listed on the label. Nothing is included without good reason. Pure essential oils act not only as natural fragrances but also as natural preservatives.

TRADITION PLUS TECHNOLOGY

The most advanced quality control processes are employed, and purity and quality are scrupulously maintained using every advantage that modern technology can provide. The most up-to-date quality controls, analytic techniques and computerised equipment are used in Weleda's laboratories.

The specialist dispensary also provides tailor-made medicines for retailers, hospitals, doctors and practitioners on a daily basis. These are special preparations to cater for individual needs, for example vegans who wish to avoid lactose-sucrose base tablets, or those who may have specific allergies.

The values which Weleda apply to their production methods are extended throughout the structure and day-to-day running of the company. A conscious responsibility towards the environment underlies every detail of operation, from the organic raising of the plants to the recyclable packaging of the end product. In many cases Weleda actually grows its own ingredients to ensure freedom from artificial fertilisers and pesticides. In fact over 300 species are grown in Weleda's Derbyshire gardens, using bio-dynamic methods.

There is a timeless quality to the philosophy which inspires Weleda products. They are essential tools in the day-to-day life of anyone who really cares about achieving total well-being, both for themselves and for their planet.

WELEDA

Weleda (UK) Ltd, Heanor Road, Ilkeston, Derbyshire DE7 8DR
Enquiries: 0115 9448200 Mail Order: 0115 9448222
http://www.weleda.co.uk

Kogan Page Ltd
120 Pentonville Road
London N1 9JN

email: kpinfo@kogan-page.co.uk

All photographs are the copyright of Mark Shearman.
The concept of this book was originated by Sport Development Resources Ltd,
Ashridge Manor, Forest Road, Wokingham, Berkshire, RG40 5SL.
Tel: 01734 795498

British Library Cataloguing in Publication Data
A CIP record for this book is available from the British Library

ISBN 07494 2260 2

Designed and typeset by Oliver Hickey

Printed and Bound in Great Britain by

Drogher Press

CONTENTS

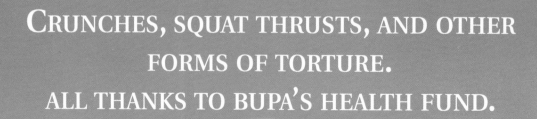

CRUNCHES, SQUAT THRUSTS, AND OTHER FORMS OF TORTURE.
ALL THANKS TO BUPA'S HEALTH FUND.

Joining a fitness club is just one of the many things BUPA's free Health Fund could help you pay for. Here's how it works.

Now when you join BUPA you can receive credits worth up to 8% of your annual membership subscription into your own personal Health Fund.

You can then choose to put your fund towards any one of a host of BUPA health care services: like membership of a BUPA approved fitness club, health screening, dental cover or even cover for long term nursing care.

Alternatively, you can let the value of your fund build up year by year, to help provide for future health needs.

Why is BUPA doing this? Because it's a provident association and it specialises in health care. So any savings we make can be passed to our members in extra health benefits.

To find out more about joining BUPA, call free today on 0800 600 500 quoting the reference below.

You're amazing. We want you to stay that way.

BUPA

THIS year BUPA celebrates its 50th birthday. The company was founded in 1947 to prevent and cure sickness as well as to promote health in any way, objectives which have remained unchanged and fit with BUPA's modern message: You're amazing. We want you to stay that way.

Athletics is a powerful expression of the wonders of the human body, promoting positive attitudes towards health and fitness.

BUPA began its involvement with British Athletics in 1993 and has recently committed its support up to the Sydney Olympic Games in 2000. With a wealth of talented young athletes beginning to make their mark, BUPA hopes to provide the platform to enable them to take the sport into the 21st century.

This year the four outdoor meetings will be known as the BUPA Series and awards are being set up to reward those who perform well consistently.

No other British company is doing more to encourage health and fitness in Britain than BUPA and 100,000 people will take part in BUPA-sponsored events this year. These include the BUPA Great Run Series (in Newcastle, Edinburgh and Portsmouth), the Fitness Industry Association's Fit For Business and Commit to Get Fit campaigns; together with healthy walking programmes along The Thames Path National Trail and junior tennis initiatives. In addition BUPA is the health care supplier to the Flora London Marathon.

Jamie Baulch

BUPA has launched a new service, *Fitness Manager,* which is designed to provide customers with a realistic and enjoyable programme that takes account of their current fitness level and helps them set goals for the future.

It involves three stages, each closely supervised by the customer's personal fitness instructor.

General health is assessed through discussion of medical history, alcohol and tobacco consumption and current level of exercise. Then the customer's current state of fitness is assessed by measuring their weight, body fat percentage, blood pressure, cholesterol, stamina and heart rate.

Also taken into account are the individual's personal goals and expectations. Is weight loss the desired result, or is building stamina and muscle more important?

Armed with this information, a personal fitness adviser will devise an exercise programme. A full fitness assessment is available annually and regular interim progress checks are recommended.

Debbie Marti

BUPA Fitness Manager builds on the links forged with 240 health and fitness clubs across the nation which are approved by the Fitness Industry Association. It is available to anyone, not just BUPA members or even of the club where their assessment takes place. The £50 fee includes a free copy of the BUPA Active Health Guide.

Steve Smith

BUPA's Amazing World

The number of people turning to the Internet for information is growing rapidly. Amazing World, BUPA's web site, includes a whole range of health information and interactive features and gives visitors access to medical advice.

Users can calculate their body mass and aerobic capacity and estimate how many units of alcohol they are drinking. They can measure physical stress symptoms and levels of stress in their workplace, receive advice about handling stress and take part in a health quiz to find out how much they know about their body.

The Ask-a-Doctor site gives specific information on common conditions and complaints from back pain, cancer and asthma while the Back Pain Forum allows people to e-mail BUPA's medical team with questions or requests for advice. Other topics available on Amazing World include information on health and exercise, dietary advice and stopping smoking.

Amazing World can be accessed on http://www.bupa.co.uk

The stylish and provocative football magazine for grown-ups

On sale every month FourFourTwo

PART ONE

1996 SEASON

JANUARY

1   Morpeth: Steve Brace starts the year by winning the Newcastle to Morpeth road race.

6   Mallusk: Kenya's James Kariuki wins over 8km in the World Cross Challenge with Chris Sweeney second. Paula Radcliffe is a convincing winner of the women's 4.8km race from Kenya's Rose Cheruiyot.

13   Luton: Middlesex's John Downes and Cheshire's Suzanne Rigg win the CAU Inter-Counties senior cross country titles.

14   Amorebieta (Spain): Kenya's Josephat Machuka beats compatriot Daniel Komen in the latest leg of the World Cross Challenge. Ethiopia's Derartu Tulu, the reigning world cross champion, wins the women's race.

20   Houston (USA): Steve Brace finishes second in the Houston Marathon in 2:10:35.

21   Seville (Spain): Ethiopia's Haile Gebrselassie splashes through torrential rain to win his only World Cross Challenge appearance of the winter. Andrew Pearson finishes seventh.

24   Budapest (Hungary): Death of Sandro Iharos who, despite a modest championship record, set world records at seven distances between 1500m and 10,000m in 1955 and 1956.

27   Birmingham: GB men beat Russia 69–68 but the women go down 57–80. Judy Oakes makes a record seventy-third GB appearance. Best performances were Jason Gardener's 6.55 60m, Tony Whiteman's 3:39.47 1500m and Dalton Grant's 2.34 high jump. Nick Buckfield sets UK indoor pole vault record of 5.50.

27   Sindlefingen (Germany): Haile Gebrselassie takes nearly ten seconds off the world indoor 5000m record with 13:10.98. Previous best was by Tanzania's Suleiman Nyambui with 13:20.4 in 1981.

28   Osaka (Japan): Germany's Katrin Dorre wins the women's marathon in 2:26.04, the fastest time of the year.

30   Perth (Australia): Emma George vaults 4.41 for her fourth women's pole vault world record.

3 Tourcoing (France): James Kariuki wins latest round of IAAF Cross Challenge but Andrew Pearson is only one second back and beats Morocco's Khalid Skah.

3–4 Birmingham: Nick Buckfield raises his indoor pole vault record to 5.61 at the AAA. Sally Gunnell returns to a British track for the first time in 16 months but has to settle for second behind Melanie Neef. Best of the rest is Mark Hylton's 46.45 400m.

4 Stuttgart (Germany): Haile Gebrselassie runs 3000m in 7:30.72, to knock nearly four seconds off the world record held by Kenya's Moses Kiptanui. Spain's Fermin Cacho sets a European record with 7:36.61 in second place.

9 Reno (USA): Canada's Donovan Bailey runs 5.56 for 50m to break the world record formerly held jointly at 5.61 by Germany's Manfred Kokot from 1973 and USA's James Sanford from 1981. After much debate about whether or not Bailey got a false start the record was finally ratified in October.

10 Birmingham: Mozambique's Maria Mutola runs 2:32.08 to break the world 1000m record held by Germany's Brigitte Kraus at 2:34.8 since 1978. Steve Smith clears 2.36 in the high jump and Ashia Hansen sets UK and Commonwealth indoor triple jump record of 14.58.

12 Tampere (Finland): Namibia's Frankie Fredericks runs an indoor 100m world best of 10.05.

12 Tokyo (Japan): Brazil's Vanderlei Lima wins Tokyo Marathon in South American record of 2:08:38 with three other men under 2:09.

18 Lievin (France): Fredericks runs a phenomenal 19.92 for an indoor world 200m record. Nigeria's Davidson Ezinwa runs an African 60m record, and world leading time, of 6.50. Burundi's Venuste Niyongabo just misses Eamonn Coghlan's indoor world 2000m mark with 4:54.76.

24 Glasgow: GB men beat France 72–67 but the women lose 69–70. Kate Staples sets UK indoor pole vault record of 3.85.

25 Stockholm (Sweden): Maria Mutola reduces her own 1000m record to 2:31.23. Steve Smith jumps 2.30 but finishes second, behind Norway's Steinar Hoen's 2.32, and just misses out on winning the Ricoh Grand Prix.

25 Diekirch (Luxembourg): Keith Cullen finishes second behind Zimbabwe's Tendai Chimusasa in the thirteenth round of the IAAF World Cross Challenge. Paula Radcliffe does likewise behind South Africa's Colleen De Reuck.

1–2 Atlanta (USA): The incomparable Michael Johnson runs a 44.66 indoor 400m and Gwen Torrence runs 200m in US record of 22.33.

3 Ashington: Keith Cullen is a convincing winner of BAF Cross Country Championships, beating Andrew Pearson by 12 seconds, with Chris Sweeney third. Alison Wyeth wins the women's race from Liz Talbot.

3 Kajaani (Finland): World indoor javelin best (!) of 85.78 by Matti Narhi.

8–10 Stockholm (Sweden): Meeting records at the European indoor championships came from Portugal's Fernanda Ribeiro over 3000m in 8:39.49 and Iceland's Vala Flosadottir clearing 4.16 in the pole vault. A gold medal for Du'aine Ladejo over 400m with silvers for Jason John at 60m and Tony Whiteman at 1500m.

10 Lisbon (Portugal): Kenya's Tegla Lorupe runs 67:12 for a half-marathon, just missing Liz McColgan's world best by a second.

14 Newark: John Nuttall and Alison Wyeth win the Reebok English National Cross Country Championships. USA's Nneena Lynch crosses the line first in the women's race but is disqualified for entry infringements and, unbeknown to all concerned, had previously failed a drug test in the USA.

23 Cape Town (South Africa): Africa dominates the World Cross Country Championships with Kenya taking a clean sweep of the team titles. Kenya's Paul Tergat retains his men's title, winning from Morocco's Salah Hissou. Jon Brown is the first non-African home in twelfth and Rob Denmark is the next Briton in forty-fifth to help the GB men finish fifth. Ethiopia's Gete Wami is the surprise winner of the women's title from the Kenyans Cheruiyot and Mugo. Paula Radcliffe finishes a disappointed nineteenth after struggling with an injury during the previous month.

24 Gyeongju (South Korea): Spain's Martin Fiz, the European and world marathon champion, runs a personal best of 2:08:25 but only beats local favourite Lee Bong-ju by a second.

25 Cape Town (South Africa): IAAF finally clear Diane Modahl after a protracted fight to clear her name of any allegations of drug taking after a 'positive' drug test at a Lisbon meeting in June 1994.

30 Milan (Italy): Paul Tergat runs 58:51 for a half-marathon, breaking the previous best by nearly a minute, although the Stramilano course is later found to be around 40m short.

APRIL

4 Lancaster (USA): Barney Ewell, the 1948 Olympic 100m silver medallist, dies aged 78.

10 Paris (France): Richard Nerurkar runs 61:06 half-marathon but finishes fourth, behind three Kenyans lead by Paul Koech in 60:31.

13 El Paso (USA): Barbados's Obadele Thompson runs the fastest ever 100m ever recorded in 9.69 albeit at high altitude and with a following wind of over 5 metres a second!

13–14 Copenhagen (Denmark): Kenya and Ethiopia win the men's and women's titles at the World Road Relay Championships. GB teams finish eighth and seventh respectively with Jon Solly running a 29:10 10km leg.

14 Johannesburg (South Africa): Iwan Thomas runs a Welsh 400m record of 44.66.

15 Boston (USA): 100th anniversary of the Boston Marathon sees Kenya's Moses Tanui win the $100,000 first prize in 2:09:15, crossing the line ahead of four of his compatriots. Germany's Uta Pippig wins the women's race for the third successive year in 2:27:12.

20 La Coruna (Spain): Spain wins both the men's 20km and 50km team competitions at the European Race Walking Cups and Italy wins the women's 10km team race. There are no British teams.

20 Sochi (Russia): Russia's Yelena Nikolayeva sets a world best of 41:04 for 10km walk at the Russian Olympic trial.

21 London: Mexico's Dionicio Ceron wins the London Marathon for the third year in a row, this time in 2:10:10. Paul Evans is the first Briton home in third with 2:10:40. Liz McColgan wins the women's race in 2:27:54.

27 Sutton Coldfield: Bingley Harriers win the Reebok National 12-stage title in 4:02:06, with the biggest ever winning margin. Next home are Tipton in 4:06:27. Fastest short stage of 13:44 was run by both Jon Solly and Darius Burrows. Richard Nerurkar runs the fastest long stage in 24:50.

28 Rotterdam (Holland): Ethiopia's Belayneh Densimo, the holder of the world best in 2:06:50 on the same circuit, wins the Rotterdam Marathon in 2:10:30 for his first marathon victory since 1990. Belgium's Lieve Slegers wins the women's race in 2:28:06.

Imperial Cancer Research Fund

Registered Charity No. 209631

The Imperial Cancer Research Fund is at the forefront of understanding cancer. The research carried out in our laboratories helps advance new ideas and new techniques for preventing, treating and curing cancer.

RACE FOR LIFE ®

5Km Walk/Run

EXCLUSIVELY FOR WOMEN

- 1 in 3 people in the UK will be affected by cancer at some stage in their lives and currently 1 in 4 will die from the disease.

- This year in Britain around 140,000 women will be diagnosed with cancer.

- The Imperial Cancer Research Fund's mission is to lead the way in saving lives through research into the causes, prevention, treatment and cure of cancer.

The Imperial Cancer Research Fund's *Race For Life* – a 5km national event series exclusively for women, where women can walk, jog or run in support of research into cancers which affect women.

The inaugural *Race For Life* was staged in 1994, in Battersea Park, London. More than 680 women took part raising over £35,000 for Imperial Cancer's life saving work. In the three years since its inception over 17,500 women have supported the *Race For Life* and over £750,000 has been raised.

One reason that the *Race For Life* is so successful is that it is an event that all women, no matter what their fitness level, can take part in and it is in support of a cause that is relevant to all.

Entry forms for the 1997 *Race For Life* series are available from the Entry Hotline. For general information on the *Race For Life* or for details on how you, your club or organisation can help the Imperial Cancer Research Fund's *Race For Life* call the *Race For Life* Team on 0171 269 3412.

Your Support can help make a difference.

Race For Life, PO Box 264, Exeter, EX4 5YZ.

Race For Life Entry Hotline: 0990 134 314

Imperial Cancer Research Fund

Race For Life...Life is for living

1997 RACE FOR LIFE VENUES

1. **DUMFRIES**
   Dock Park 2.00pm 11/5/97

2. **LEEDS**
   Roundhay Park 11.00am 11/5/97

3. **BRISTOL**
   Clifton Down..................... 11.00am 18/5/97

4. **MANCHESTER**
   The Velodrome 11.00am 18/5/97

5. **MILTON KEYNES**
   Emberton Park 11.00am 18/5/97

6. **EDINBURGH**
   Holyrood Park 2.00pm 1/6/97

7. **GUERNSEY**
   Footes Lane........................ 11.00am 1/6/97

8. **PRESTON**
   Moor Park 11.00am 1/6/97

9. **LONDON**
   Battersea Park 7.30pm 4/6/97

10. **GLASGOW**
    Queens Park........................ 2.00pm 8/6/97

11. **MIDDLESBROUGH**
    Acklam Sports Centre........... 11.00am 8/6/97

12. **PETERBOROUGH**
    Thomas Cook Leisure
    Centre 7.00pm 11/6/97

13. **HULL**
    City Centre........................ 11.00am 15/6/97

14. **MAIDSTONE**
    Mote Park 11.00am 15/6/97

15. **DUNDEE**
    Camperdown....................... 2.00pm 22/6/97

16. **NORWICH**
    University of East Anglia.... 11.00am 22/6/97

17. **PLYMOUTH**
    City Centre....................... 11.00am 22/6/97

18. **ABERDEEN**
    Hazlehead Park 2.00pm 29/6/97

19. **GUILDFORD**
    Stoke Park 11.00am 29/6/97

20. **NEWCASTLE**
    Newburn Country Park 11.00am 29/6/97

21. **BRIGHTON**
    Preston Park 11.00am 6/7/97

22. **LONDON**
    Hampstead Heath................ 11.00am 6/7/97

23. **CARDIFF**
    Bute Park 7.00pm 9/7/97

24. **SHEFFIELD**
    Don Valley............................ 7.00pm 9/7/97

25. **JERSEY**
    The Esplanade, St. Hellier... 11.00am 13/7/97

26. **OXFORD**
    University Parks.................. 11.00am 13/7/97

27. **BIRMINGHAM**
    Sutton Park........................ 11.00am 20/7/97

28. **SOUTHAMPTON**
    The Royal Victoria
    Country Park........................ 11.00am 20/7/97

29. **CHELTENHAM**
    Pittville Park 11.00am 27/7/97

30. **NOTTINGHAM**
    Forest Recreation Ground... 11.00am 27/7/97

31. **RICHMOND**
    Richmond Park.................... 11.00am 27/7/97

32. **LINCOLNSHIRE**
    RAF Cranwell 11.00am 3/8/97

(ALL RACES UNDER BAF PERMIT)

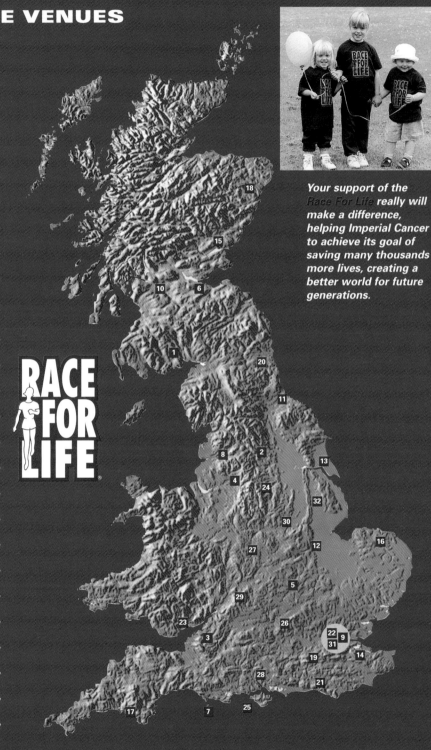

Your support of the Race For Life really will make a difference, helping Imperial Cancer to achieve its goal of saving many thousands more lives, creating a better world for future generations.

RACE FOR LIFE

Imperial Cancer has the best scientists and doctors pushing back the boundaries of research into the causes and treatment of cancer. We're incredibly optimistic about the next few years - by building on what we already know, our vision of being able to prevent, treat or cure many cancers can and will be achieved. Please help us by supporting Race for Life.
Entry Hotline: 0990 134 314

5   Cleveland (USA): Kenya's Joseph Kimani sets 10km world road best of 27:20.

12   Cluj (Romania): Romania's Mihaela Melinte throws 69.42 for a women's hammer world record.

12   Arnsburg (Germany): Linford Christie makes his European outdoor debut and wins over 100m in 10.20.

15   Wythenshawe: Diane Modahl makes her competitive return, over 800m, since being sent home from the 1994 Commonwealth Games.

18   Bedford: Tessa Sanderson returns after four years in retirement and throws 60.64, an Olympic qualifying standard and world over-40 record.

18   Atlanta (USA): Inaugural meeting on the Olympic track sees Gwen Torrence zip to a 10.85 100m and Russia's Sergey Bubka clears a 1996 best of 6.02 in the pole vault. Jonathan Edwards wins the triple jump with a windy 17.59.

18/19   Istanbul (Turkey): Belgrave Harriers finish third in the men's European Champions Cup. Victories for Du'aine Ladejo over 400m and Nigel Bevan in the javelin.

25/26   Gotzis (Austria): Syria's Ghada Shouaa wins the heptathlon at the annual multi-event classic in a world leading 6942 points. Denise Lewis is second in a UK record 6645 points.

25   Cardiff: Jon Ridgeon runs under 50 seconds for the 400m hurdles after returning from injury, and for the first time since 1992, with 49.87.

25   Jena (Germany): Czech Jan Zelezny throws a javelin world record of 98.48.

26–27   Bedford: Hammer thrower Dave Smith provides the highlight of the CAU Inter-Counties Championship with a 75.10 throw.

26   Ljubljana (Slovenia): Darren Braithwaite runs 10.14 100m and Kate Staples sets UK pole vault record of 3.90.

28   Bratislava (Slovakia): 100m win for Darren Campbell in 10.17 and a rare victory for Tony Jarrett over Colin Jackson in the 110m hurdles, 13.24 to 13.27.

1/2 Madrid (Spain): Linford Christie posts a sprint double of 10.04 and a windy 20.25 at the European Cup Super League. The 100m was a record seventh consecutive victory in the competition and a Cup record. Other men's victories for Jonathan Edwards with a windy 17.79 triple jump and the 4x400m quartet with 3:03.38. Women's victories from Sally Gunnell with 56.84 in the 400m hurdles and Ashia Hansen with a 14.57 triple jump. The only other Cup record comes from Spain's Roberto Parra with a 1:44.97 800m. Germany win both men's and women's competitions. GB men finish second and the women sixth.

3 St Denis (France): Frankie Fredericks runs 9.95 100m.

5 Rome (Italy): Four men run inside 13 minutes in a 5000m won by Salah Hissou in 12:50.80.

7 Moscow (Russia): John Regis wins Grand Prix 200m in 20.47.

14–23 Atlanta (USA): Michael Johnson runs 200m in 19.66 at the US Olympic trials to break the longest standing world record in a championship event. He also runs a 43.44 400m. Other highlights included Allen Johnson's 110m hurdles in 12.92, Kenny Harrison's windy 18.01 triple jump, Dan O'Brien's 8726 decathlon and Gwen Torrence's 10.82 100m.

14–16 Birmingham: Roger Black sets a UK 400m record of 44.39 at the AAA Championships, which double as the Olympic trials. Nick Buckfield emulates Black in the pole vault with 5.71. Christie equals his 100m season best of 10.04 but loses 200m to John Regis with both men timed at 20.54. Jon Ridgeon runs a 49.16 400m hurdles, Tessa Sanderson throws a world over-40 record of 62.88 and Debbie Marti high jumps 1.94.

19 Stockholm (Sweden): Sweden's Edvin Wide, the oldest surviving Olympic medallist and five times a world record holder in the 1920s, dies aged 100.

25 Helsinki (Finland): Frankie Fredericks speeds to 9.87 100m with Darren Braithwaite second in 10.13. Jonathan Edwards triple jumps 17.82.

28 Paris (France): Tony Whiteman runs 3:34.47 but has to settle for fifth place behind Noureddine Morceli's 3:29.50. Linford Christie finishes third in the 100m behind the Canadian pair of Bruny Surin and Donovan Bailey.

29 Reims (France): Emma George improves her own women's pole vault world record to 4.42.

30 Gateshead: Steve Backley secures his Olympic place with a javelin throw of 81.66 at the BUPA Games, but finishes behind the USA's Tom Pukstys. Angie Thorp runs a windy 12.95 100m hurdles and Australia's Cathy Freeman produces the highlight of the meeting with a 49.96 400m, with Sally Gunnell second in 51.45.

JULY

3   Lausanne (Switzerland): Frankie Fredericks runs 9.86 100m into the wind with Christie fifth in 10.05. Other highlights include a new Commonwealth 200m record by Trinidad's Ato Boldon in 19.85; Michael Johnson's 43.66 400m with Roger Black second in a new UK record of 44.37 (Mark Richardson runs 44.52 for second in the B race!) and France's Marie-Jose Perec's 49.45 over the same distance. Sally Gunnell pulls up injured in the 400m hurdles won by the USA's Tonya Buford-Bailey in 53.61.

4   Atlanta (USA): Joseph Kimani runs world best road 10km in 27:04.

5   Oslo (Norway): Fredericks beats Johnson over 200m at Bislett Games, winning in 19.82 to 19.85. Algeria's Noureddine Morceli wins Dream Mile in 3:48.15 with John Mayock third in 3:50.32. Jonathan Edwards triple jumps 17.68, Francis Agyepong is second with 17.18. Ireland's Sonia O'Sullivan runs 1500m in 3:59.91 while Portugal's Fernanda Ribeiro wins the 5000m in 14:41.07, the fastest time of the year.

8   Stockholm (Sweden): Kenya's Daniel Komen, not selected for Atlanta, runs 5000m in 12:51.60 with Jon Brown tenth in 13:20.10. Morocco's Hicham El Guerrouj becomes the sixth 1500 man to run under 3:30 with his 3:29.59.

10   Nice (France): Denmark's Wilson Kipketer runs 800m in 1:42.51, the fastest for 11 years. Noureddine Morceli runs 2000m in 4:49.55. Sonia O'Sullivan wins the Grand Prix 3000m in 8:35.42, the fastest time of the year.

12   London: Jonathan Edwards jumps 17.52 at the Securicor Games and Steve Backley produces an 85.58 throw in the javelin. Sanderson throws the woman's implement 64.08 while Cathy Freeman produces a 49.59 400m.

12–13   Sheffield: Nathan Morgan long jumps a windy 7.97 at the TSB English Schools Championships, the longest leap of the year by a Briton.

13   Rudingen (Germany): USA's Randy Barnes puts the shot 22.40, the furthest for six years.

14   Lappeenranta (Finland): Daniel Komen sets world two miles record of 8:03.54, breaking Haile Gebrselassie's record by nearly four seconds.

OLYMPICS 27 July – 4 August

Atlanta (USA): World records from Donovan Bailey with 9.84 100m and the amazing Michael Johnson, who runs 200m in 19.32. Spare a thought for Frankie Fredericks who ended up with two silver medals despite running 9.89 and 19.68. Johnson had previously won the 400m in 43.49, nearly a second in front of silver medallist Roger Black.

Africa take all the men's gold medals from 1500m upwards. Haile Gebrselassie wins an outstanding 10,000m duel from Paul Tergat while Josia Thugwane's marathon triumph is South Africa's first gold medal since the end of apartheid.

In the field, Carl Lewis takes his fourth long jump title while Kenny Harrison produced a triple jump of 18.09, the second best ever, to snatch the title from Jonathan Edwards and defeat him for the first time in 23 competitions. Edward's 17.88 is the best ever leap not to win a competition.

Overdue Olympic golds for Noureddine Morceli and the USA's Dan O'Brien but an upset in the steeplechase where Moses Kiptanui is beaten by his compatriot Joseph Keter.

Marie-Jose Perec follows in Johnson's footsteps and wins the 200m and 400m in 22.12 and 48.25. Russia's Svetlana Masterkova notches up an 800m and 1500m double in 1:57.73 and 4:00.83. Ethiopia's Fatuma Roba wins the marathon in 2:26.05 with a winning margin of exactly two minutes. The winning times of Fernanda Ribeiro, in the 10,000m with 31:01.63, and Jamaica's Deon Hemmings in the 400m hurdles with 52.82, are the best in the world for the year.

Exceptional field event performances come from Russia's Inessa Kravets with a 15.33 triple jump and Germany's Ilke Wyludda's 69.66 discus throw. Steve Backley takes the silver medal in the javelin with 87.44, but gold goes to Jan Zelezny with 88.16.

The 4x400m quartet of Iwan Thomas, Jamie Baulch, Mark Richardson and Roger Black also take a well-deserved silver medal in a European record of 2:55.60. There are bronze medals for high jumper Steve Smith and heptathlete Denise Lewis, the only one by a British woman at the Olympics. Fourth place finishes came from Colin Jackson in the 110m hurdles, Kelly Holmes over 800m and Ashia Hansen in the triple jump. Angie Thorp set a UK 100m hurdles record in her semi-final. Linford Christie is disqualified from the 100m final after two false starts.

10 Monte Carlo (Monaco): Daniel Komen runs 3000m in 7:25.16, just missing Noureddine Morceli's world record. Wilson Kipketer runs a 1:42.59 800m while Svetlana Masterkova win's the women's event in 1:56.04. Paula Radcliffe finishes third in the 3000m in 8:37.07 behind winner Romania's Gabriela Szabo.

11 Crystal Palace: Ashia Hansen sets new UK and Commonwealth triple jump record of 14.67 at the Performance Games. Steve Backley throws 82.10.

14 Zurich (Switzerland): Svetlana Masterkova runs a women's mile world record of 4:12.56 at the Weltklasse meeting while Daniel Komen again just misses the 5000m mark, this time with 12:45.09, but beats record holder Gebrselassie. German throwers Lars Riedal and Raymond Hecht throw the discus and javelin 71.06 and 92.28 respectively. Jonathan Edwards wins the triple jump with a stadium record 17.79.

16 Cologne (Germany): Paula Radcliffe finally beats Zola Budd's UK 5000m record with 14:46.76, finishing fifth in the Grand Prix race won by Gabriela Szabo in 14:44.42.

17 Kingston: Sale Harriers win the GRE British League for the first time, beating holders Belgrave Harriers on a tie-break of event points.

19 Gateshead: Linford Christie's last international match but he is beaten into second in the 200m by John Regis's run of 20.62. Roger Black runs a 44.64 400m and Jonathan Edwards jumps 17.35.

21–24 Sydney (Australia): Bulgaria's Tereza Marinova sets the only world record of the World Junior Championships with a 14.62 triple jump. Other names to look out for in the future are Nigeria's Francis Obikwelu, who won gold medals over 100m and 200m, and Ethiopia's Assefa Mezegabu, who did likewise over 5000m and 10,000m. Britain notches up four silvers from 800m man Tom Lerwill, high jumper Ben Challenger, decathlete Dean Macey and 400m hurdler Vikki Jamison. Bronze medals go to long jumper Nathan Morgan and the men's 4x400m quartet.

23 Brussels (Belgium): Salah Hissou reduces the world 10,000m record to 26:38.08, taking more than five seconds of Gebrselassie's 14–month–old mark. His compatriot Hicham El Guerrouj improves Said Aouita's Moroccan 1500m record to 3:29.05 in a race in which John Mayock finishes sixth in 3:33.94. Svetlana Masterkova break's Maria Mutola's world 1000m mark with 2:28.98.

25 Cleder (France): Carolyn Hunter-Rowe wins the European 100km title in 7:41.29 and the women's team wins the bronze medal.

25 Sheffield: Billed as Linford Christie's last ever international meeting. He finishes third over 100m, behind Davidson Ezinwa and Ian Mackie, the first British sprinter to beat Christie in a 100m final since 1986. Ashia Hansen improves her own UK and Commonwealth triple jump record to 14.78 but has to settle for second behind Czech Sarka Kasparkova's 14.84.

30 Berlin (Germany): Frankie Fredericks, Wilson Kipketer, Jonathan Edwards, Lars Riedal and Stefka Kostadinova share twenty gold bars after winning all four Golden Four events, the prize is worth around $32,000 each. Edwards jumps 17.69.

31 Hendon: Belgrave Harriers win the GRE Gold Cup with Birchfield Harriers taking the women's GRE Jubilee Cup.

THE PRE-SCHOOL LEARNING ALLIANCE

For further information please contact:
Jon Marsh,
Fundraising Section,
Pre-school Learning Alliance,
69 Kings Cross Road,
London WC1X 9LL

Tel: 0171 833 0991
Fax: 0171 837 4942

The Pre-school Learning Alliance, a registered educational charity, is the single largest provider of care and education for children under-five in England. Founded in 1961, pre-schools began when parents, frustrated by the lack of nursery provision for their young children, took matters into their own hands by creating their own self-help nursery schools. Today, 800,000 children under five attend the 20,000 pre-schools in membership of the charity in England, including 60% of three-year-olds and nearly 30% of four-year-olds.

Pre-schools are run by trained staff, have a distinctive educational culture and involve the participation of parents. The Pre-school Learning Alliance has its own recommended curriculum guidelines which were approved by the then Department for Education in 1991. The charity provides the only voluntary Accreditation Scheme, which offers a 'kitemark' for pre-schools offering very high standards of education and care.

The Pre-school Learning Alliance has as its main fundraising campaign the Pre-school Child Appeal, which aims to raise money to subsidise the pre-school fees of children from low income families and children with special needs. Of the 800,000 children attending pre-schools, 200,000 need financial help. Only a tiny fraction receive any grants from their local councils and, without the charity's own fundraising, many of these children would miss out altogether on pre-school education.

The Pre-school Learning Alliance is the single largest organisation providing quality education and care for under-fives in England.

The Alliance is a registered educational charity and has:

- Nearly 20,000 pre-schools in membership.
- Nearly 800,000 children attending these pre-schools.
- Nearly one million families involved with the pre-school movement.
- Parental involvement which research has shown benefits children's education and development.
- A pre-school curriculum.
- More than 50,000 student enrolments on training courses.

69 Kings Cross Road, London WC1X 9LL

Telephone: 0171 833 0991
Childcare Helpline: 0171 837 5513

1   Rieti (Italy): Daniel Komen finally gets an official world record with a 7:20.67 3000m. Statisticians have worked out that this equates to two back-to-back four-minute miles. Wilson Kipketer runs 1:41.83, the fastest 800m in 12 years. Noureddine Morceli wins 1500m in 3:29.99 with John Mayock seventh in 3:33.34.

7   Milan (Italy): Daniel Komen and Sweden's Ludmila Engquist are the overall Grand Prix champions, taking home $250,000 each, the richest ever prize in athletics history. Jamaica's Merlene Ottey is faster than ever at 36, running a 10.74 100m and Hicham El Guerrouj becomes the first man in four years and 46 races to beat Noureddine Morceli over 1500m or a mile. Jonathan Edwards wins $150,000 by taking the triple jump with 17.59 and finishing second in the men's overall standings. Best British women's performance comes from Paula Radcliffe, fourth in the 5000m with 14:56.36.

9   Sarajevo (Bosnia): John Mayock wins 2000m at International Meeting of Solidarity in 5:00.91, beating Salah Hissou.

14   Telford: Janine Whitlock sets new UK pole vault record of 4.00

15   Newcastle: Kenya's Benson Masya wins the Great North Run in 61:43, his fourth victory. Paul Evans finishes second in 61:55. Liz McColgan makes up for her Atlanta disappointment and wins women's race in 70:58

16   Tokyo (Japan): Wilson Kipketer runs 1:42.17 for 800m and Germany's Astrid Kumbernuss, the Olympic shot put champion, completes an unbeaten season but Svetlana Masterkova loses for the first time in 1996, over 800m to Cuba's Ana Quirot. Jonathan Edwards losses to Kenny Harrison, 17.51 to 17.38. Steve Backley finishes third in the javelin, won by Jan Zelezny with 89.32, but throws 84.46.

22   Amsterdam (Holland): Kenya's Josephat Machuka sets 10 miles world best of 45:18.

29   Palma (Spain): Italy's Stefano Baldini wins the world half-marathon title in 61:17 and leads his country to the team gold medals with Dave Swanston first Briton home in twenty-second. GB men finish eleventh. China's Ren Xiujuan wins the women's race in 70:39 with Romania taking the women's team title for the fourth year in succession. Liz McColgan drops out at 16km. First Briton home is Sally Goldsmith in twenty-ninth and the GB women finish ninth.

29   Berlin (Germany): Spain's Abel Anton wins the Berlin Marathon on his debut in 2:09:15 while Colleen De Reuck wins the women's race in 2:26:35.

OCTOBER

6   Portsmouth: Gary Staines wins the BUPA Great South Run in 46:57; his third victory on the trot. Ethiopia's Derartu Tulu wins the women's race in a course record 52.39 with Marian Sutton second in 52:53.

6   Solihull: Eamonn Martin and Hayley Haining win Nike BAF 10km titles in 29:01 and 33:25.

20   Chicago (USA): Paul Evans wins the Chicago Marathon in 2:08:52 with Eamonn Martin fourth in 2:11:21 and Gary Staines fifth in 2:11:25. Marian Sutton takes the women's race in 2:30:41.

26   Sutton Coldfield: Bingley Harriers win the Nike National six-stage with Richard Nerurkar running the fastest stage in 16:15. Birchfield Harriers win the women's four-stage relay with Zara Hyde running the fastest leg in 14:20.

NOVEMBER

3   New York (USA): Italy's Giacomo Leone and Romania's Anuta Catuna win the New York Marathon in 2:09:54 and 2:28:18.

10   Margate: Neil Caddy wins the Margate International cross country event.

17   Tokyo (Japan): Japan's Nobuko Fujimura wins the Tokyo Women's Marathon in 2:28:58 with Liz McColgan third in 2:30:50.

23   Gateshead: Spencer Barden wins Safeway Cross Country with Andrea Whitcombe winning the women's race.

23   Chiba (Japan): GB men finish second behind South Africa in the Chiba International Ekiden.

DECEMBER

8   Llodio (Spain): Jon Brown beats Paul Tergat by 15 seconds to win the Llodio cross country.

10   Melbourne (Australia): Emma George sets new world indoor pole vault record of 4.40

15   Cherleroi (Belgium): Brown becomes the first British man for twenty-one years to win an international senior cross country title when he romps home at the European Championships by 35 seconds from Paulo Guerra, the defending champion who helps Portugal retain their title. The men finish fifth as the women, led by Hayley Haining in ninth, win the bronze team medals. Romania, led by winner Iulia Negura, once again take the title.

Why is the *Minimal Bounce Bra*® and **M.A.N**™ the most important pieces of sports equipment a woman and man can wear?

A Story of Guts,

Scots delight: Black wins Commonwealth gold in Edinburgh.

FOUR PAGES further on from a national newspaper feature last November dealing with the proposed British Academy of Sport began a three-page focus on Southampton University Medical Sport. How fortunate for us, the British athletics fan, that Roger Black was relevant for interview with connection in the first article, rather than the second.

To trace how close athletics came to being untouched by Black's many and varied qualities we must go back to 1984, to a failed maths A level. Until then he had been a team sports player, rugby mainly. 'I was always a good athlete – the fastest in Hampshire – but it did not appeal,' he said. The signpost on his career path pointed towards following his father into medicine.

But the failed maths exam forced a delay and, to fill in time, he gave athletics a shot. 'Messing up maths meant I had to retake before I could read medicine,' he said. 'During that time a close friend, who was an athlete, invited me to train with him.' Thus began a story of guts, gold and glory.

Belatedly, Black enrolled in the med-ical programme at Southampton University but he left after one term. His instant success on the track in 1985, when he won the European junior 400 metres title, was a blood sample of the embryonic superstar athlete. So he abandoned his studies to concentrate on preparing full-time for the 1986 Commonwealth Games.

Interruptions, interruptions

By the end of 1986, aged only 20, Black was Commonwealth and European champion, British record hold-er too with 44.59secs. Then the salt spilt into his wine. A hamstring injury in 1987 restricted him to the relay at the World Championships in Rome and a stress fracture in his right foot put him out of the 1988 Seoul Olympic Games.

Interruptions, interruptions. Always, for Black, interruptions. After winning the European title in 1990, and world silver in 1991, he was not fully fit for the 1992 Olympics, later requiring surgery on a badly aligned hip, and he missed the 1993 World Championships in

Full flow: Black in Atlanta

30

Gold and Glory...

tuttgart after falling victim to the debili-
ating Epstein Barr virus, described by
lack as 'crippling lethargy'.

At the 1992 Olympics in Barcelona,
David Grindley set a British record to
each the final, a performance which
enied Black a place in the final eight.
Whispers that Black's day was past started
p. 'I heard that one or two athletes
were saying, "he's bottled it", particularly
when David Grindley was doing so well.'

Lacking background training for the
1994 season, Black was denied a third
uccessive European title by fellow
riton Du'aine Ladejo and, though he
eached the final of the 1995 World
Championships in Gothenburg, he fin-
hed seventh. Suffering torn knee carti-
age, a lesser character might have been
empted to call it a day. Not Black.

He spent £9000 on surgery, taking
is tally of operations to four. Then, final-
y, he had an uninterrupted run into a
eason. After setting two British records,

44.39secs in the British Olympic trials in
Birmingham and 44.37 in the Lausanne
Grand Prix, he went to the Atlanta
Games in ebullient mood. 'This sport is
not difficult when you are healthy,' he
said. His Olympic silver medal, with only
Michael Johnson finishing ahead of him,
was, he said, 'the best thing I have ever
done.' He also collected a relay silver to
go with his World, European and
Commonwealth relay golds.

Motivation

Black, typical of the man's resourceful-
ness, turned adversity to advantage.
One of his many sidelines is corporate
speaking, motivation his theme. 'My
problems have given me a good story
to tell that seems to go down very well,'
he said.

The multi-talented Black talks with
mouth, feet and fingers. Words of motivation for the businessman, the fastest
size 13s you are likely to see, fingers

Smiling happy people: Olympic silver

strumming songs he has composed
himself on the guitar. He plays chess. He
has been a team captain on BBC television's 'A Question of Sport'. He has presented sports news on BBC South and
written a regular column for 'The Times'.
He was a prime mover in the formation
of the British Athletes' Association, which
has been given power by the British
Athletic Federation to help in commercial negotiations on behalf of the sport.

Look up at the map for the place
where wisdom meets beauty and you
will find Roger Black. Tall, 6ft 3in, lean,
muscular, elegant. One female daily
newspaper columnist observed: 'He has
looks that make women walk into lamp
posts.'

He was voted Ultimate Sex on Legs In
Sport by a teenage girls' magazine in
1992 and topped a Who Would You
Most Like to Shack Up with poll in a
women's magazine. Britain's athletics
writers voted him a wow, too, making
him their 1996 male athlete of the year.

ecord run: Black regains the UK record

Relaxing in California

'He was a prime mover in the formation of the British Athletes' Association, which has been given power by the British Athletic Federation to help in commercial negotiations on behalf of the sport.'

- Born: March 31st, 1966, Portsmouth
- Club: Team Solent
- Gold medallist, 1986 and 1990 European Championships
- Winner 1986 Commonwealth Games
- Member of 4x400m relay team that won 1991 World Championships
- 1996 Olympic silver medallist 400m and 4x400m relay
- Silver medallist 1991 World Championships

PROGRESSION AT 400M

1984 47.7	1991 44.62
1985 45.36	1992 44.72
1986 44.59	1993 45.86
1987 44.99	1994 44.78
1988 -	1995 44.59
1989 46.2	1996 44.37*
1990 44.91	

*(UK Record)

Bambi: Black proves he is a thoroughbred with European gold 86

It is hard to grasp now that Black once had a take-it or leave-it attitude towards athletics. There was a time when he declined to compete for Hampshire in the English Schools Championships because it clashed with him singing in his school's production of 'The Mikado'. 'If you had asked me at 17 or 18 what my ambitions were I would have said to represent England in rugby,' he said.

Black was an England Schools triallist as a winger and the comparison with Eric Liddell is unavoidable. Liddell, a winger, played rugby for Scotland and won the 1924 Olympic 400 metres title. Liddell, too, was the son of a doctor. On the sportsfield, Black did not match Liddell's achievements but it is a more competitive world in which we live today and one can only wonder what Liddell would have made of Michael Johnson.

onker

his early years as an athlete, Black was
cknamed 'Bambi' because his legs had
tendency to go wobbly. He did not
ways judge his races well and, after
nning the 1990 European gold medal
Split, he admitted that he had run a
oor tactical race. 'I am a plonker but a
onker with a gold medal round my
eck,' he said, acknowledging that he
d kicked too early and that he was for-
nate that he had held on at the finish.

A lesson that you are soon forgotten
me his way in 1994 when, on his
ird comeback, his first race for almost
year, he ran the 200m in a British
ague Division Five match in Sheffield.
the athletes went to their marks, the
adium announcer ran the line-up. The
all crowd waited for mention of the
iropean champion in lane three.

Then it came. 'In lane three, Roger
ark, Team Solent.' Black did not take
fence. 'Who is that mystery man?'
ack, alias Clark, responded. Down the
ome straight, leading by three metres
ll the commentator was calling him
oger Clark. Reassurance, though, that
remained a public figure came when
returned to the opposite side of the
adium to collect his tracksuit.

chor: Black leads the relay team to another
tory

Yes! Celebrating in Atlanta

'Get your vest off Rog,' a young mother
shouted.

Black has always been forthright in
his opinions, not least when several top
British athletes were told to prove their
fitness for the 1995 World
Championships. 'Madness,' he said.
'There are European, Olympic and
World champions among us and we
are being treated like children.' When
Ladejo dampened Black's British record
celebrations at the Olympic trials, by saying that he would not hold the record

for long, Black's indignant response was
to strike a £1000 bet with Ladejo that
he would not run 44.39 in 1996. Black
won the bet.

Barring serious injury, Black may continue through to the 2000 Sydney
Olympics and certainly until 1998,
when he will be 32 and seek to regain
his European title. 'There is Life After
Surgery,' a headline on the
Southampton Medical School feature
article said. It could just as easily be used
to headline Black's life story in athletics.

Denise Lewis

Thanks: Lewis with her Mum Joan and coach Daryl Bunn

LEWIS IN THE DRIVING SEAT

Denise Lewis's bronze in Atlanta made her the first British female multi-eventer since Mary Peters t[o] win an Olympic medal. But as TREVOR FRECKNALL, of 'Athletic[s] Weekly', discovered things nearl[y] turned out very different

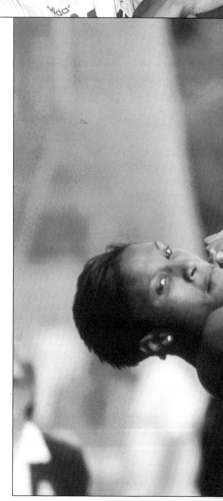

DENISE LEWIS entered a pretty exclusive Hall of Fame in Atlanta last July.

She became only the third British woman to win an Olympic multi-event medal – and you can grasp the size of the achievement from the fact that both the other two were pocketed before she was born.

It's so long since Mary Rand struck silver in 1964 and Mary Peters grabbed gold in 1972, they were restricted to five disciplines – although Rand also won the long jump in Tokyo to confound the athletics masters' theory that the girls were as delicate as the crino-lines they were trying to shake-off, figuratively speaking; and Peters has become the president of the British Athletic Federation to explode the other ancient myth, that female athletes should be seen but never heard.

In all seriousness, though, Lewis would have finished eighth instead of third in Atlanta if she'd had to call a halt after five events.

As it is, her heptathlon bronze medal was a richly earned reward for a thoroughly modern Ms – a

'All I want to do at the end of the competition is come back home and say, "You gave it your best shot."'

interview

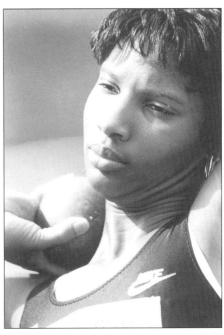

Heavyweight: Lewis is now the World No. 2

tting room-mate for the Common-wealth Games gold earned in equally dramatic circumstances two years earlier.

But it's what happened in between these major triumphs that sets Denise Lewis apart from most of her contemporaries – especially those who seem to have been persuaded that improvement is hopeless without financial support from the Government, the National Lottery, Uncle Peter Radford and all.

In November 1995 she literally made a meal of self-help. At the 'Birmingham Post and Mail' Sports Personality of the Year Dinner, she was placed at a table with representatives from seven distinctly non-sporting businesses – insurers, computer programmers, auction-

eers, motor sellers – and signed them up to sponsor her through to the Sydney Olympics in the year 2000. 'Denise absolutely captivated us,' said Mark Bevan, one of the group she inevitably calls 'My Magnificent Seven'.

Each of them agreed to back her to the extent of £1000 per year. Not a lot in an era when footballers earn more than that per minute. But it's a queen's ransom for a young Midlander whose dedication to her sport prohibited her from working any longer than part-time for a pittance during the hard years when she really needed help.

The rhetorical question now is: Does Britain – the Government, the National Lottery, Uncle etc, etc – realise her value?

Born on 27 August 1972 in West Bromwich, she still acknowledges her most important sponsor has been her mum, Joan. 'She's always been strong,' said Denise. 'My best friend and biggest sup-

porter. And sometimes she'll get the scrapbook out and ask, 'Did my little Denise do that?"'

Which probably explains what went through Denise's fevered brain at the 1994 Commonwealth Games. She entered the competition as her country's (and club's No 2 to Clova Court). After a mighty javelin personal best of 53.68 metres, she was suddenly in the gold medal position with one event to go. 'I didn't want to go out for that 800,' she recalled, eyes widening at the terrifying prospect a year and more on. 'My first reaction was, "I'm still a baby." I felt such an amazing wave of emotion. I wanted to cry.'

Walking out onto the track at the University of Victoria, she focussed on the lessons instilled at junior school, at Wolverhampton & Bilston AC, at Birchfield Harriers... by her school teachers, her first coach Bill Hands who 'taught me the basics – good habits' and her present coach Darryl Bunn, whose final pre-race instruction was to the point: 'Run your heart out!' She did. A pb of 2:17.60 earned her the gold medal by just eight points, the smallest winning margin in Games history. The reigning champion, Australian Jane Flemming, departed in tears of disbelief with her silver medal.

One of Denise's first ports of call on her return home was to her junior school. It was there that she maybe began to grasp the magnitude of her achievement. 'People I didn't know were coming up to me with tears in their eyes, saying "Well done!" One dinner lady was so happy for me, she was in floods of tears.'

There were more tears last July in Atlanta. Her own. Day One had been desperate. Day Two had started with another disaster, 6.32m in the long jump, her best event. She sat sobbing. 'I really didn't think I could solve anything,' she said. 'I was in despair out there.'

No amount of funding from the Government, the National Lottery, etc, etc, could have brought what happened next.

Physiotherapist Kevin Ludlov and her coach sat beside he Listening to her. Talking to he 'Darryl has looked after me since was 14 or 15,' she said after th Commonwealth triumph – addin prophetically, 'He has helped m maintain the dream.'

● ● ● ● ● ● ● ● ● ● ● ● ● ● ●

Getting the point: Lewis's javelin has improved greatly

On that hot and humid 28 Jul in Atlanta, he suggested she sta the dream. 'If it's upsetting you sc drop out,' he suggested. 'You're i this sport for enjoyment. There always another day.'

Reverse psychology? Genuin concern? Call it both. It gav Denise the incentive to gather he jumbled thoughts, restore he serene self-confidence... remembe the principles on which she ha built her career from the time sh was an Under-13 a Wolverhampton & Bilston.

She's always been very clea that 'I can't stomach people wh quit. If you drop out after one ba event, what can you learn abou the event or yourself? If you dro out once, it's easier to drop ou the next time things are not goin absolutely right. You have to b true to yourself.'

So she stepped back into th pressure cooker called Centennia adium and, in her own words, lo and behold, the javelin came o my rescue again.' Her third nd final throw speared out to 4.82m, a pb by over a metre, nd moved her from eighth to hird.

For an encore, she ran the

Alas, the feat had gone largely unnoticed in the UK. Maybe if she'd knocked Nightshade off a perch with an oversize feather duster at the National Indoor Arena, Birmingham, during a recording of 'The Gladiators' she'd have received more recognition.

It's a pity the TV cameras and directors couldn't have popped into one of the Birmingham primary schools in which Lewis worked part-time on the city council's community education programme.

Denise admits her arrival was a terrible anti-climax for the children, whose excitement was such that they rushed into the playground to await the arrival of the Commonwealth champion. They were obviously unimpressed as she climbed out of her VW Polo, a vision in her sponsor's lycra.

'She can't be a champion,' piped up an eight-year-old. 'She's not got a limousine.'

Denise smiles. 'My first athletics lesson was to explain to them that British champions don't drive limousines – not many of them, anyway.'

They don't. They drive themselves. With the help of coaches like Darryl Bunn. And mums like Joan Lewis. And most of all, with philosophies like Denise Lewis's. 'All I want to do at the end of the competition is come back home and say, "You gave it your best shot."'

Which begs the question to the Government, the National Lottery, Uncle etc, etc: What's the going rate for a national inspiration?

● ●

- **Born: August 27th 1972, West Bromwich**
- **Club: Birchfield Harriers**
- **Gold medallist, 1994 Commonwealth Games**
- **1996 Olympic bronze medallist**
- **7th place, 1995 World Championships**
- **1995 European Cup winner**

PROGRESSION AT HEPTATHLON	PERSONAL BESTS		
1989 5277	200m	24.44	1996
1990 5193	800m	2:17.60	1994
1991 5484	100mh	13.18	1996
1992 5812	HJ	1.84	1996
1993 5774	LJ	6.67	1995
1994 6325	SP	14.36	1996
1995 6299	JT	56.50	1996
1996 6645 (UK record)			

00m fast enough (2:17.41) to old-off the 1993 World Student ames champion Urszula Vlodarczyk from Poland for the ronze medal behind the world hampion Ghada Shouaa, the yrian who had improved from wenty-fifth in the Barcelona Olympics to a seemingly unassailble position, and the 1992 World unior champion Natalya azanovich, who secured silver vith a long jump pb of 6.70m at bout the moment Denise was lescending into her pit of despair.

Denise returned home the new golden girl of British athletics. And hrugged off suggestions she hould have gone to Atlanta as he new golden girl of British athetics as she had broken Judy impson's ten-year-old UK heptathlon record by scoring 6645 oints on 25–26 May at rainy Gotzis, an Austrian town that everes multi-eventers.

The fact that Judy Simpson is Nightshade is doubtless incidental to the masses of the population reared by TV to believe there have been only a handful of British athletes worth watching in the 1990s.

Versatile: In action at the AAA Championships

Although the sheer scale and over-commercialisation of the Games attracted press criticism, as did transport arrangements and computer problems, the athletics programme of the Centennial Olympics in Atlanta was nothing short of superb. The competition was great, performances outstanding with many events being the best ever in depth. The weather was kinder than expected and the number of spectators was unprecedented; more than 80,000 turned up for the first morning session and the total attendance soared to over 1,170,000.

That wasn't the only Olympic record. All 197 countries within the Olympic movement were represented at the Games, and far more nations than ever before came away with medals: 45 as against the previous highest of 35 in Barcelona in 1992. The number of countries claiming Olympic champions rose to 24. Not surprisingly, the USA was the most successful team with 23 medals, 13 of them gold.

The failure of the British team to win a gold medal attracted much media attention. IAN CHADBAND, the athletics correspondent of *The Sunday Times*, puts things into perspective

WE ARE a demanding lot. A generation used to gorging on the world-beating exploits of everyone from *Coe* to *Ovett*, from *Sanderson* to *Gunnell*, from *Thompson* to *Christie*, has come to expect British gold almost as some sort of divine right

False start . . . Linford Christie was disqualified

handed down from Mount Olympus. So when Atlanta came around and, one-by-one, our athletics victory hopes were gone with the wind, the sense of anti-climax was acute.

And, lo, the weepin' and wailin' did commence. At an Olympics where, pitifully, only one British triumph could be celebrated, that of the incomparable oarsman, *Steve Redgrave* and his partner *Matthew Pinsent*, the track and field team's failure to strike gold was pounced upon as representative of the general malaise. Tortured analysis of Britain's reduction to third-world sporting power followed. 'Why have we become also-rans?' screamed the headlines.

If you listened to the doom mer chants, Britain's entire track and field campaign in Atlanta could be defined by a few depressing image from the Centennial Stadium. *Linford Christie* standing there wild-eyed at the start line, arguing with a man in a hat who was telling him two strikes and you're out; *Sally Gunnell* being scraped up off the track by two officials; *Jonathan Edwards* gazing mournfully heavenwards after his big toe had half-inched over the triple

Silver Lining . . . Jonathan Edwards celebrates his silv

Openers . . . The opening ceremony was a glittering affair and included (top right) Muhammed Ali

ump board; *Liz McColgan* being poleaxed by a pesky insect, *Tony arrett* being flattened by some pesky hurdles.

Okay, so there can be no argument that the tale of no golds and six medals, particularly the demise of the 'holy trinity' of *Christie, Gunnell* and *Colin Jackson*, the purveyors of unprecedented major championship success these past four years, was a disappointment. Only three months earlier, *Peter Radford*, the executive chairman of the British Athletic Federation, had been ambitiously outlining 20 British medal prospects.

Calamitous Games

But perspective was needed, and found sadly lacking in many of the panic-stricken dispatches from Georgia. Yes, overall, it was a calamitous Games for British

sport, but the success of the athletics team did not need to be measured on gold alone.

Here is an alternative set of images to ponder.

Denise Lewis, with that last-gasp, lifetime best javelin throw

MIRACLE . . . Steve Backley recovered from injury to take second.

and that gut-wrenching 800m run, earning heptathlon bronze when it had seemed impossible; *Steve Backley* courageously returning to the javelin fray just months after

MEDAL TABLE

	Gold	Silver	Bronze	Total
USA	13	5	5	23
Russia	3	6	1	10
Kenya	1	4	3	8
Germany	3	1	3	7
Jamaica	1	3	2	6
Gt Brit.	0	4	2	6
France	3	0	1	4
China	1	2	1	4
Nigeria	1	1	2	4
Ethiopia	2	0	1	4

HIGH ACHIEVER ... Steve Smith maintained his great championship record.

he had been on crutches following an Achilles op to nearly topple the great *Jan Zelezny*; *Roger Black* winning the 'other' 400m race behind *Michael Johnson* while a kid called *Iwan Thomas* also tantalisingly sniffed a medal before fading to fifth.

There was *Steve Smith* rising to the occasion as ever to become the first Englishman to win a high jump medal; there was *Mark Richardson*, who could not even land a place in the individual 400m, running the fastest leg of the relay final, 43.62sec, to lead our quartet to a new European record and silver medal.

There were, as *Gunnell* commented after injury had ended her own hopes of defending her 400m hurdles crown, 'a hell of a lot of quality performances with exciting new people coming through. I don't think we've done too badly at all.'

To a point, the statistics bear her out. Judged against our performances in recent Games, Atlanta was not so different. If you accept that golds for *Gunnell* and *Christie* in Barcelona were what made for a memorable Games for Britain, that should not conceal the fact that

POOKY ... There were plenty of reminders about the games history.

The overall medal tally was the same in both Games. In Seoul, we were also gold free and, going back beyond Los Angeles and Moscow where medals came cheaper because of the boycotts, our medal tally was four in 1972 and just one in 1976 – and that in an era where the strength of the global competition was not half as ferocious as today.

Certainly, the figures cannot conceal that this was our least

CAPTAIN COURAGEOUS ... Kelly Holmes battled bravely against injury.

successful Games since *Brendan Foster's* solitary bronze spared our blushes in Montreal. Most depressing was the fact that, compared to 28 top eight finishes in Seoul and 20 in Barcelona, this time there was only 13, an alarming drop but one which has to be judged in an era when more countries than ever before, pumping more resources into the sport than ever before, shared the spoils like never before.

Substantial government backing

In total, a record 45 countries won athletics medals in Atlanta; in Barcelona, it was 35. This is the age when a Syrian woman, *Ghada Shouaa* can be crowned the world's greatest all-round female athlete, when a walker from Ecuador, *Jefferson Perez*, can win his country's first ever medal, when a Norwegian 800m man, *Vebjorn Rodal*, can run from a snow-covered mountain tunnel to Olympic gold, all supported with more substantial government backing than any British athlete could hope for.

In the ever-expanding global athletics village, the danger signs

for Britain are there all right, as *Malcolm Arnold*, our national coaching director has long pointed out, but Atlanta also delivered plenty of reasons for encouragement.

BRITISH FINALISTS AT A GLANCE

MEN

Linford Christie	100m	dsq
Roger Black	400m	2nd
Iwan Thomas	400m	5th
John Mayock	1500m	11th
Jon Brown	10,000m	10th
Paul Evans	10,000m	dnf
Richard Nerurkar	Marathon	5th
Colin Jackson	110mh	4th
Steve Smith	High Jump	3rd
Jonathan Edwards	Triple Jump	2nd
Steve Backley	Javelin	2nd
Mick Hill	Javelin	12th
4x400m	Relay	2nd

WOMEN

Kelly Holmes	800m	4th
Kelly Holmes	1500m	11th
Paula Radcliffe	5000m	5th
Liz McColgan	Marathon	16th
Ashia Hansen	Triple Jump	4th
Judy Oakes	Shot Put	11th
Denise Lewis	Heptathlon	3rd
	4x100m Relay	8th

For a start, even some of those of our rival European nations who pump far more resources into athletics fared worse. Much was made of how much we could learn from the generously funded French, Italian and Spanish systems, yet Spain won just two medals, Italy four and, while *Marie-Jose Perec* and *Jean Galfione* landed three golds for France, their overall total was also just four.

And one should not underplay the extent to which the British team was beset by wretched luck. What if *McColgan's* ankle had not swollen up like a balloon after she had been nipped by an insect – some brave insect to take on the feisty one, it has to be said – just before the marathon?

What if *Kelly Holmes*, fourth in the 800m and eleventh in the 1500m, had not been cruelly struck by a hairline fracture of her

The present and the future ... Roger Black (left) and the success of Iwan Thomas means British 400m running has never been healthier.

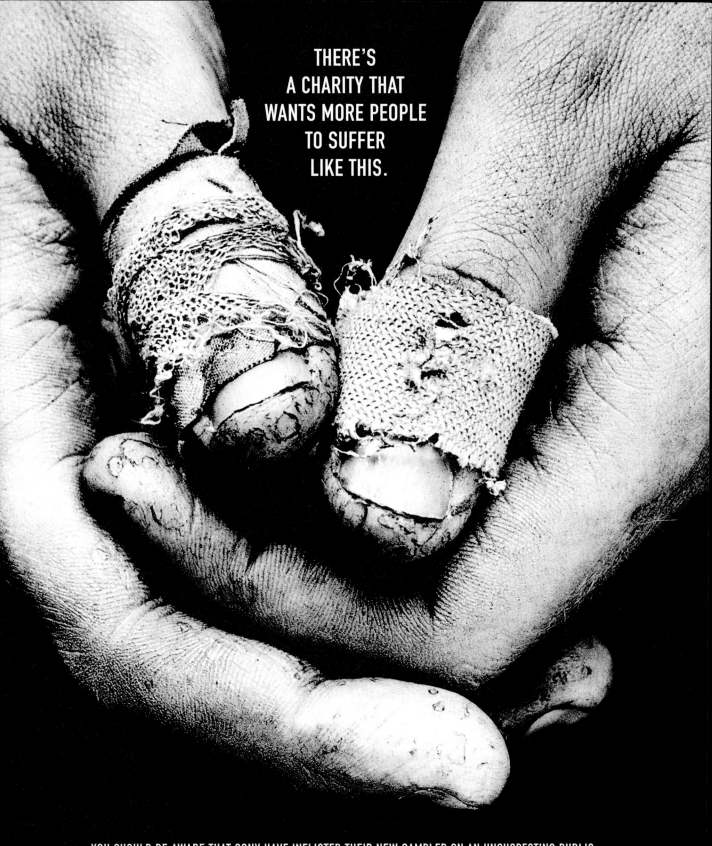

THERE'S
A CHARITY THAT
WANTS MORE PEOPLE
TO SUFFER
LIKE THIS.

YOU SHOULD BE AWARE THAT SONY HAVE INFLICTED THEIR NEW SAMPLER ON AN UNSUSPECTING PUBLIC.
POWER SOURCE CONTAINS: TOMB RAIDER, PORSCHE CHALLENGE, MONSTER TRUCKS 2 AND DESTRUCTION DERBY 2.
YES, YOUR THUMBS WILL HURT, YOUR BRAIN WILL HURT, BUT YOUR SOUL WILL BE PURE.
ALL PROCEEDS GO TO THE PRINCE'S TRUST, PROVIDING TRAINING, EDUCATION, FINANCIAL ASSISTANCE, PERSONAL DEVELOPMENT
AND BUSINESS START-UP ADVICE TO HELP YOUNG PEOPLE HELP THEMSELVES. TO FIND OUT MORE, CALL 0800 842 842.

FOOD OF WINNERS . . . The relay squad celebrate their silver medal.

that the defending champion deliberately got himself disqualified to spare himself a hammering did not understand his nature. *Christie* can be accused of many failings, but he has never shirked any challenge just because the odds were against him. Put simply, he gambled and lost.

His farewell was messy; competitors and off-track critics alike condemned his stubborn reluctance to accept referee *John Chaplin's* disqualification verdict which held up the re-run for ten minutes, but if they did not approve of his behaviour, surely they could understand the utter frustration of an Olympic champion deprived in such dramatic circumstances of even the opportunity to defend his title.

So, *Christie's* time is up at this level – at least, that's what he tells us – but the feeling that we were in on the changing of the guard came with the sight of *Ian Mackie* an unemployed lad from Dunfermline reaching the 100m semis before a hamstring injury rudely interrupted his progress. Nobody should tag the lad with the unenviable burden of being the 'new Christie', but his progress was such that, by the end of the summer, he had become the first Briton in a decade to beat the man himself over 100m. Perhaps *Christie* saw a bit of himself in this strapping Scot because it was not long before he decided to snap up *Mackie* for his Nuff Respect stable.

left shin in the weeks preceding the Games and had not had to battle through a diet of injections, ice and pain to reach her two finals?

What if *Jackson's* knee troubles had not flared up again on the day of the sprint hurdles final?

What if those two final monster leaps by triple jump silver medallist *Edwards*, which were surely beyond *Kenny Harrison's* winning mark of 18.09m, had not been ruled marginal fouls?

And the biggest 'what if' of all. What if *Christie*, after his first false start in the 100m final, had kicked out of the blocks second time around just over a hundredth of a second slower than he actually did, thus rising with the gun instead of fractionally jumping it?

Christie the gambler

It would be facile to suggest he could have matched *Donovan Bailey's* world record surge, but those who suggested spitefully

SPEED KING . . . Donovan Bailey broke the world record in the 100m.

he can see it in the shape of his 4x400m teammates; of *Thomas*, of *Richardson*, of *Jamie Baulch*. 'I can't control these little b******s,' he joked, wondering if they'll be churning out the laps over a decade like he has done, wondering indeed if he might still be around himself in Sydney four years hence to pester them.

'It might not have been the greatest of Games for us, plenty of things went wrong but we live in a culture where it's easy to always blame someone or something else for lack of success. In the end, it's down to the individual. The success has to come from within. It may be a changeover period, but new stars are on the rise.'

Perhaps the real message from Atlanta was that, frankly, we should not give a damn for defeatist talk. In those little Bs pursuing *Black*, in the ambitious likes of *Thorp* and *Mackie*, in the never-say-die likes of *Backley* and *Holmes*, we could see enough to make us remember that, as the lady said, tomorrow is another day.

IN THE SOUP . . . Paula Radcliffe ran a brave race against Wang Junxia (left), the turtle-eating Chinese star.

Inspired

Gunnell saw her Olympic crown slip in equally miserable circumstances but, even hobbling around on crutches, took her captain's role to heart by persuading *Angela Thorp*, a youngster who had undergone knee surgery just five months earlier, to go out there and break her national 100m hurdles record. Suitably inspired, *Thorp* sliced two-hundredths of a second off *Gunnell's* venerable mark of 12.82sec. *Thorp* was 24, *Mackie* just 21.

The future is far from bleak. *Smith*, *Thomas*, *Lewis*, triple jumper *Ashia Hansen* and 5000m runner *Paula Radcliffe*, top six finishers all, were under 24. 'It's a period of change, I'm sure, but I don't think we took a step backwards in Atlanta,' said *Black*, whose star has never shined quite so bright now he has joined the thirty-somethings.

'The driving force for ten years from a success point of view was *Linford*. Nobody can immediately fill his shoes, but there's always talent – you can see it.'

A glance over his shoulder, and

Help the Aged

Dash for Cash...

Why not set yourself the ultimate challenge and take part in the New York City Marathon®?

Organisers of one of the UK's premier 10K road races - **the Leeds Abbey Dash** - the Charity's Leeds based SportAge department also organises 5K road races, fun runs, duathlons, triathlons, and a national series of junior and senior mountain bike events for athletes of all ages and abilities.

The proceeds benefit older people in need across the world.

For further information, including an event schedule please contact SportAge on Tel: 0113 279 6000.

For information about the New York City Marathon® please contact Special Events on Tel: 0171-253 2926.

SportAge supports Help the Aged by raising funds through organising sports and leisure activities.

Help the Aged is a company limited by guarantee
Registered in England No. 1263 4466
Registered Charity No. 272786
Registered office: St James's Walk, London EC1R 0BE

FASTAID OFFERS RELIEF FROM SPORTING INJURIES

Top athletes like Roger Black MBE, recognise and understand the benefit of using specific products like Cool X, to prevent pain and further damage to sports injuries. FastAid offers a range of products to specifically target the requirements of sportsmen and women. Fastaid Cool X, Blister Plasters, Heat Pad and Relief-Xtra all provide effective solutions to many common sports injuries.

Cool X provides immediate long lasting ice cold relief for up to six hours for bruises, sprains and strains. The cooling gel pad is available as a 14cm x 10cm thin adhesive plaster, which can be moulded to the body direct from the pack, with no need for refrigerator or freezer storage, for ease of use.

Understanding the need for specific blister protection, FastAid have produced Blister Plasters to target the treatment of blisters. Blister Plasters have been designed using a hydrocolloid pad to draw the moisture from the blister and thereby aid careful healing. Made from soft polyurethane material the plasters are highly comfortable and conformable, and adhere to the skin using a low allergy acrylic adhesive. Once a blister has developed, FastAid Blister Plasters provide suitable cushioning and protection of the wound preventing further rubbing and infection.

When muscular aches and pains need therapeutic warmth FastAid Heat Pads are a convenient source of warmth lasting up to five hours. The adhesive pads are comfortable and discreet to wear, even during exercise, and are odourless and free from drugs and chemicals.

A natural remedy for persistent aches and pains is available using FastAid Relief-Xtra, a natural remedy for persistent aches and pains using magnetic therapy. Passed down from the Chinese and ancient Egyptians, magnetic therapy is believed to increase blood flow, relaxing muscle or tissue and reducing pain where the magnet is applied.

Relief-Xtra magnetic discs, worn discreetly in the form of small circular plasters, apply the beneficial effects of magnetic force stimulations to give relief from pain be it through a sporting injury or a long term chronic condition. They are particularly useful for the relief of persistent niggling pain using magnetic therapy as the secret of its success.

ROGER BLACK AND
Fast Aid COOL-X
A WINNING COMBINATION

Developed with the needs of sportsmen and women in mind Fast Aid Cool - X is an adhesive cooling gel pad which can be used on injuries immediately and without the need for refrigeration.

Cool - X moulds to the shape of the body and provides long lasting cold action for up to 6 hours .

Just the thing to reduce swelling, aid healing and get you back in action as soon as possible.

Make sure you are fully prepared this season - ask for Fast Aid Cool - X at your local chemist or drugstore.

A complete range of First Aid products

THE FIRST TWO YEARS

AFTER two seasons of the TSB Rankings, it can now be said that they accurately reflect the current overall performances in British Athletics.

The TSB Senior Rankings will tell you that Richard Nerurkar is the top male distance runner ahead of Paul Evans and that Simmone Jacobs is marginally better than Katharine Merry in women's sprinting. They would also tell you that Ian Mackie is twenty-ninth and Janine Whitlock is twelfth, and while those positions may provoke some debate that, of course, is a primary objective – to create interest and discussion on the relative merits of athletes from different events.

The TSB Rankings may seem complicated with their requirements of a minimum number of performances achieved within a set period, coupled with bonus points for major championship placings and records. However, their format bears a similarity to those successfully adopted in tennis, golf and cricket.

The tables used to calculate the points values, which have been continually monitored for inconsistencies, can now be compared very favourably with the IAAF's own tables, yet adjustments will continue to be made as and when the standard of any event changes.

Looking ahead, the principal objectives of the TSB Rankings will be for them to remain topical and gain a greater understanding from the athletes themselves.

SURF THE NET!

THE success of the TSB Junior Rankings has given rise to their own particular problems. All junior athletes now want to see their position on the ranking list. But, even with a specific publication such as this, it is not practical to print the names of 1000 athletes in each of the six age groups.

Internet to the rescue!

By using a comprehensive web site it has been possible to provide full on-line listings of the of the TSB Junior Rankings. Along with this there is also so much more available, including the TSB Senior Rankings, profiles of top athletes with photographs, full results from the last two years' TSB English Schools' and Olympic results.

This is only the start! Look out for announcements of additions to the TSB web site in the coming year. It will continue to be the premier athletics site on the web. Internet web site address: http://www.tsb.co.uk

BLACK SCALES THE HEIGHTS

Roger Black reflects on his season-long rise up the 1996 TSB Senior Rankings

SINCE the beginning of the 1995 athletics season when he was ranked thirteenth on the TSB Senior Rankings, Roger Black has risen ten places to No 3 behind Steve Backley in second and Jonathan Edwards in first.

The impressive rise reflects an outstanding season for Roger, in which he set two British records over 400m and which culminated in two silver medals at the Olympic Games.

Still basking in the glow of his successes, Roger gave *The British Athletics Annual* his thoughts on the TSB Rankings. 'I'm pleased to see how well the TSB Rankings have reflected my performances,' he said.

Thanks to the fine-tuning which has occurred since they were launched in 1995, the TSB Senior Rankings present an accurate picture of last season. 'It is also good to see that four of my 400m team-mates are now in the top-20 TSB Men's Rankings, which show the strength in-depth of the squad.

'The TSB Junior Rankings are definitely one of British Athletics' success stories of recent years. They continue to enjoy tremendous support from young athletes who enjoy seeing how their performances rank them against their peers.
'The TSB Junior Rankings are a great motivator for Britain's juniors, whether they're ranked fifth or 500th.

'It is extremely rewarding for a young athlete to see how a personal best can dramatically move them up the tables. It is also amazing how many youngsters know exactly where they rank and how a split second's difference in their time can affect their rankings score.

'I will watch with interest how the TSB Rankings progress over the next few years and would like to see them provoke as much interest and debate as they have done to date.

'The TSB Rankings undoubtedly add a new and exciting dimension to British Athletics, which is always good for the sport.'

BANKING ON THE FUTURE... TOP JUNIORS

✪ JAMIE HENTHORN, 19
Pembrokeshire College

JAMIE was fourth in the World Junior 100m final as well as winning both Welsh U20 sprint titles and setting a Welsh Junior record over 200m indoors.

am really pleased at being TSB's top male Welsh athlete of the ...ason and am quite surprised to be No 1 on the TSB Welsh ...nior Rankings.

...e had a lot of help from my coach Steve Perks, and feel I've ...ne really well after being injured at the start of the season.

...he highlight of the summer was finishing fourth in the World ...hampionships in Sydney in 10.47secs. This performance must have ...ally boosted my ranking.

...he TSB Rankings show athletes what to aim for and are an extra ...centive to do well. I think they are particularly good for the ...unger age groups as they give them an added challenge.'
...B Welsh Ranking: 1

REBECCA ROLES, 16
Neath College

...EBECCA improved the Welsh U17 pole vault record from 2.90m ... 3.20m. She finished second in the Welsh AAA Championships ...d won the TSB Welsh Schools' and U17 discus titles.

...m really chuffed to have been chosen as the TSB Welsh athlete of ...e season and am also pleased to hear that I am in third place on ...e TSB Welsh Junior Rankings. This is an added encouragement to ...ntinue with athletics and to be ranked in the top 100 against the ...glish and Scottish juniors in the near future.

...'s interesting to see how I compare to all other athletes in my ...e group – I think the TSB Rankings are a good idea.'
...B Welsh Ranking: 3

RICHARD McDONALD, 16
Perth High School

...CHARD'S season began with victory in the AAA U17 indoor ...iple jump and ended with a win over 800m at the McDonald's ...ames. He broke the UK 400m hurdles record and won the AAA ...d TSB Schools' international titles. He also ran 48.59 in the ...0m and won the TSB SAF U20 400m hurdles title.

...am extremely pleased to be top Scot and to be fourth on the ...B Rankings against all the Scottish, Welsh and English athletes of ...y age group. I could not have had a better summer... I didn't fall ...ver a single hurdle!

...he TSB Rankings have added an extra element of competitiveness ...r athletes which can only be good for the sport. They also give ... a laugh when we can see how fast we need to run to equal Carl ...yerscough's ranking points!'
...B Junior Ranking: 4
...B Scottish Ranking: 1

KIMBERLEY CANNING, 14
Carluke High School

..."S been a great year for Kimberly with TSB Scottish Schools' and

SAF titles over 200m. She also clocked a personal best of 25.07 for 200m to win the AAA English crown. Kimberley's previous pb pre-1996 was a wind assisted 26.14.

'I can't believe I am No 1 on the TSB Scottish Junior Rankings and sixth on the TSB British Junior Rankings. I am also really surprised at being selected as the top Scottish junior athlete of the season.

'The TSB Rankings are a great idea and I always like to see where I am ranked after a good performance. The TSB Rankings unit is really popular at events and it is fun to compare yourself against your friends.

'I also like the way they tell you what you need to run or jump before you will be ranked No 1 in Britain.'
TSB Junior Ranking: 6
TSB Scottish Ranking: 1

✪ CARL MYERSCOUGH, 17
Millfield School

CARL attained previously unheard of distances in the shot and raised the UK U17 record from 19.22m to 21.20m. He is the 1996 TSB English Schools' and AAA Indoor champion and won the U20 outdoor titles at both shot and discus.

'I am really delighted that I have been nominated for the top English male junior athlete of the season. I've obviously got a long way to go but this shows I'm definitely going in the right direction.

'I think the TSB Rankings are a good idea and fair to all athletes. I'm quite surprised to be No 1 but it's a great honour. I think it's quite unusual for a field athlete to do so well, but I have had to work hard for it.

'I'd like to say well done to all the other junior athletes who have trained just as hard as me and are also doing well on the TSB Rankings.'
TSB Ranking: 1

✪ FIONA HARRISON, 14
Pope Pius School

IN only her second season of pole vaulting, Fiona was the No 3 teenager in Britain, clearing 3.50m. She won four AAA U15 titles – 100m, long jump outdoors, 60m and long jump indoors.

'I'm really excited and pleased to be No 1 on the TSB Rankings and to have been selected the top female junior athlete in England. I've been really pleased with my performances and hope that this is the start of something big to come.

'I think the TSB Rankings are a great idea and everyone I know is interested to see where they are ranked against their friends and competitors. It is also useful to know how much faster you need to run etc to be ranked No 1. It gives you something to aim for.'

TSB Rankings: 1

1996 MEN'S AND WOMEN'S RANKINGS

Men Pos		Points	Women Pos		Points
1	Jonathan Edwards	1483.25	1	Kelly Holmes	1353.25
2	Steve Backley	1384.75	2	Paula Radcliffe	1327.00
3	Roger Black	1352.00	3	Denise Lewis	1316.00
4	Colin Jackson	1343.75	4	Ashia Hansen	1310.50
5	Linford Christie	1318.75	5	Liz McColgan	1270.50
6	Steve Smith	1306.00	6	Sally Gunnell	1234.25
7	Tony Jarrett	1282.00	7	Judy Oakes	1220.00
8	Iwan Thomas	1241.75	8	Angela Thorp	1213.00
9	John Regis	1226.50	9	Phylis Smith	1166.50
10	Mark Richardson	1217.75	10	Debbie Marti	1163.75
11	Du'aine Ladejo	1217.50	11	Tessa Sanderson	1158.75
12	John Mayock	1217.00	12	Janine Whitlock	1154.00
13	Anthony Whiteman	1216.00	13	Diane Modahl	1152.25
14	Jonathan Ridgeon	1211.75	14	Simmone Jacobs	1149.50
15	Francis Agyepong	1203.00	15	Katharine Merry	1141.25
16	Mick Hill	1199.00	16	Marian Sutton	1139.75
17	Nick Buckfield	1194.50	17	Lea Haggett	1132.25
18	Richard Nerurkar	1188.00	18	Diane Allahgreen	1132.25
19	Jamie Baulch	1187.75	19	Lorraine Shaw	1127.50
20	Dalton Grant	1186.00	20	Jacqui Agyepong	1127.25
21	Bob Weir	1183.25	21	Louise Fraser	1126.25
22	Darren Braithwaite	1180.75	22	Donna Fraser	1124.50
23	Nick Nieland	1174.75	23	Michelle Griffith	1124.50
24	Paul Evans	1172.75	24	Jacqui McKernan	1123.50
25	Justin Chaston	1171.25	25	Alison Wyeth	1122.25
26	Jon Brown	1170.25	26	Sonia McGeorge	1119.75
27	Keith Cullen	1167.75	27	Lyn Sprules	1119.00
28	Curtis Robb	1158.50	28	Sue Parker	1118.25
29	Ian Mackie	1157.50	29	Kate Staples	1116.00
30	Andrew Tulloch	1156.75	30	Karen MacLeod	1115.50
31	Darren Campbell	1155.75	31	Alison Layzell	1113.25
32	Peter Crampton	1150.75	32	Sonya Bowyer	1111.50
33	David Strang	1149.25	33	Sally Goldsmith	1110.25
34	Craig Winrow	1146.75	34	Beverly Kinch	1110.00
35	David Smith	1143.75	35	Marcia Richardson	1107.75
36	Rob Denmark	1142.50	36	Louise Brunning	1107.50
37	Doug Turner	1141.25	37	Vicki Lupton	1105.25
38	Shaun Pickering	1138.25	38	Melanie Wilkins	1104.50
39	Paul Gray	1137.25	39	Paula Thomas	1104.50
40	Glen Smith	1136.00	40	Vikki Jamieson	1104.00
41	Neil Owen	1135.25	41	Lorraine Hanson	1103.25
42	Kevin McKay	1133.50	42	Stephanie Douglas	1103.25
43	Gary Cadogan	1133.50	43	Heather Heasman	1101.00
44	Owusu Dako	1132.50	44	Louise Watson	1100.25
45	Colin Mackenzie	1131.25	45	Alison Curbishley	1100.00
46	Gary Lough	1131.25	46	Angie Hulley	1097.50
47	Paul Head	1128.25	47	Shelley Holroyd	1096.50
48	Jason John	1127.75	48	Lynn Gibson	1096.25
49	Peter Whitehead	1127.50	49	Lucy Elliott	1094.00
50	Matt Simson	1124.25	50	Sam Farquharson	1093.50

1996 JUNIOR RANKINGS

Men Under-20

Pos		County	Event	Points	Performance	Venue	Date
1	James Brierley	Shrops	HJ	1122	2.26	Nembro	3 Aug
2	Tom Lerwill	Essex	800	1106	1:47.27	Sydney	22 Aug
3	Dwain Chambers	Mx	100	1092	10.42	Bedford	27 Jul
4	Ross Baillie	Scwest	110H	1092	14.01	Sydney	25 Aug
5	Damien Greaves	Essex	110H	1087	14.04	Sydney	25 Aug
6	Kevin Nash	Surrey	3ks/c	1083	8:43.21	Cr Palace	2 Jun
7	Corri Henry	Notts	400	1083	46.50	Sheffield	13 Jul
8	Jamie Henthorn	Dyfed	100	1083	10.45	Sydney	22 Aug
9	Ben Challenger	Leics	HJ	1078	2.21	Sydney	24 Aug
10	Nathan Morgan	Leics	LJ	1076	7.97w	Sydney	13 Jul
11	Tom Mayo	W Mids	1500	1074	3:43.4	Loughborough	5 Jun
12	Sean Baldock	Sussex	400	1065	46.80	Birmingham	14 Jun
13	Dean Macey	Essex	DEC	1060	7480	Sydney	22 Aug
14	Anthony Gill	W Yorks	110H	1058	14.11w	Sheffield	13 Jul
15	Uvie Ugono	London	100	1052	10.55	Bedford	27 Jul
16	Ben Warmington	Northumb	110H	1048	14.18w	Sheffield	13 Jul
17	Brendan Smith	G Man	1500	1047	3:45.6	Stretford	16 Jul
18	Michael Tietz	Derby	100	1046	10.57	Ljubljana	28 Sep
19	Geoff Dearman	Mx	400	1045	47.0	Nembro	3 Aug
20	C Robertson-Adams	Shrops	400H	1044	52.26	Birmingham	15 Jun

Women Under-20

Pos		County	Event	Points	Performance	Venue	Date
1	Vikki Jamieson	NI	400H	1115	57.27	Bedford	28 Jul
2	Susan Jones	G Man	HJ	1091	1.87	Sheffield	12 Jul
3	Michelle Dunkley	Northants	HJ	1072	1.85	Sheffield	12 Jul
4	Rachael Forest	Shrops	HJ	1072	1.85	Bedford	27 Jul
5	Natasha Danvers	Kent	100H	1069	13.74	Bedford	28 Jul
6	Rhian Clarke	Suffolk	PV	1066	3.70	Hendon	10 Aug
7	Victoria Shipman	Derby	100	1055	11.5	Nembro	3 Aug
8	Lesley Owusu	Berks	400	1047	54.53	Loughborough	19 May
9	Michelle Mann	Lancs	3000	1047	9:30.5mx	Stretford	25 Jun
10	Denise Bolton	G Man	100H	1044	13.95	Bedford	28 Jul
11	Emma Symonds	Norfolk	400	1040	54.6	Nembro	3 Aug
12	Malgorzata Rostek	Scwest	100	1039	11.83	Katowice	7 Jul
13	Ellen O'Hare	Gloucs	800	1038	2:06.59	Nembro	3 Aug
14	Kate Williams	M Glam	400H	1037	60.21	Hendon	10 Aug
15	Rebecca Drummond	Staffs	100	1033	11.86	Bedford	27 Jul
16	Tracey Duncan	Mx	400H	1030	60.47	Hendon	10 Aug
17	Julie Pratt	Essex	100H	1028	14.08	Bedford	28 Jul
18	Liz Fairs	Derby	100H	1026	14.10	Bedford	28 Jul
19	Philippa Roles	W Glam	DT	1019	51.38	Belfast	22 Jun
20	Shelly Ann-Bowen	Berks	100	1017	11.95	Sheffield	12 Jul

Men Under-17

Pos		County	Event	Points	Performance	Venue	Date
1	Carl Myerscough	Lancs	SPY	1232	21.20	Blackpool	22 Sep
2	David Parker	N Yorks	JTY	1053	73.56	Stoke	20 Jul
3	Christian Linskey	S Yorks	PV	1035	5.15	Sydney	23 Aug
4	Richard McDonald	Sceast	400HY	1021	52.81	Pitreavie	10 Aug
5	Luke Davis	W Mid	100	1016	10.44w	Sheffield	13 Jul
6	Kris Stewart	Sceast	400	1009	47.6	Nembro	3 Aug
7	David Naismith	Derby	400	991	48.05	Hendon	10 Aug
8	Ben Lewis	W Mids	200	987	21.66	Ljubljana	28 Sep
9	Martin Lloyd	Kent	HJ	983	2.10	Eltham	28 Sep
10	David Readle	Mersey	SPY	980	16.89	Birmingham	18 Aug
11	Carl McMullen	Ches	400HY	977	53.8	Stoke	20 Jul
12	Edward Coats	Surrey	OCTY	977	5158	Worcester	25 Aug
13	Luke Rosenberg	Herts	DTY	975	51.30	Birmingham	8 Sep
14	Jon Heggie	Derby	400HY	961	54.2	Stoke	20 Jul
15	Colin McMaster	Scwest	HJ	957	2.07	Stoke	20 Jul
16	Richard McNabb	S Yorks	400	953	48.71	Sheffield	13 Jun
17	Alloy Wilson	Essex	400	953	48.71	Birmingham	8 Aug
18	David O'Leary	Mersey	100HY	952	13.16w	Sheffield	13 Jul
19	Tim Kitney	Bucks	JTY	951	65.92	Pitreavie	10 Aug
20	Chris Carson	Sceast	200	950	21.93	Birmingham	17 Aug

Women Under-17

Pos		County	Event	Points	Performance	Venue	Date
1	Sarah Claxton	Essex	LJ	1043	6.24	Mannheim	15 Jun
2	Sarah Wilhelmy	Essex	200	1033	24.25	Bedford	28 Jul
3	Amanda Pritchard	Card	800	1026	2:07.32	Belfast	22 Jan
4	Katherine Livesey	Lancs	HEPI	1023	4830w	Birmingham	22 Sep
5	Danielle Freeman	W Yorks	HEPI	1018	4801	York	23 Jun
6	Chloe Cozens	Beds	HJ	1015	1.79	Sheffield	13 Jul
7	Nicola Hall	Suffolk	80HI	1014	11.41	C Palace	30 Jun
8	Sarina Mantle	Essex	80HI	1014	11.25w	Sheffield	13 Jul
9	Jade Johnson	London	LJ	1012	6.08	Tooting Bec	28 Apr
10	Rebecca White	Lancs	300	1006	39.25	Birmingham	17 Aug
11	Helen Roscoe	Ches	200	1005	24.39w	Sheffield	12 Jul
12	Katy Lestrange	Ches	80HI	1004	11.47	Sheffield	12 Jul
13	Maria Bolsover	S Yorks	300	1003	39.32	Sheffield	12 Jul
14	Ruth Watson	Cambs	300	1002	39.34	Sheffield	12 Jul
15	Yewande Ige	Surrey	300H	1001	43.08	Sheffield	13 Jul
16	Abiodun Oyepitan	Mx	100	998	12.06	Birmingham	17 Aug
17	Wendy Cox	Durham	200	992	24.38w	Sheffield	13 Jul
18	Rachael Kay	G Man	300H	988	43.2	Stretford	8 Jun
19	Lindsay Impett	Dorset	300	988	39.66	Sheffield	12 Jul
20	Dionne Howell	London	200	988	24.43w	Sheffield	13 Jul

Men Under-15

Pos		County	Event	Points	Performance	Venue	Date
1	Matthew Sutton	Staffs	HTB	914	63.64	Stoke	22 Jun
2	Ken McKeown	Scwest	HJ	905	2.01	Pitreavie	10 Aug
3	John Barnes	Humber	HTB	883	61.32	Hull	8 Jun
4	Richard Lainson	Hants	JTB	877	60.34	Birmingham	18 Aug
5	Daniel Angus	Cleve	200	855	22.65	Sheffield	12 Jul
6	Rhys Williams	Dyfed	JTB	854	58.58	Pitreavie	10 Aug
7	Joe Brown	London	100	843	11.28	Sheffield	12 Jul
8	Seb Bastow	Cleve	80HB	842	11.10	Sheffield	13 Jul
9	Damien Howard	Norfolk	HTB	837	57.84	Sheffield	13 Jul
10	Aaron Evans	Kent	400	832	50.88	Birmingham	17 Aug
11	Ross Thompson	Durham	HTB	830	57.28	Jarrow	8 Jun
12	Tim Benjamin	S Glam	100	829	11.33	Swansea	6 Jul
13	Andrew Rose	Essex	100	829	11.33	Sheffield	12 Jul
14	Tristan Anthony	Herts	200	826	22.63w	Sheffield	13 Jul
15	Jonathan Lundman	Essex	JTB	824	56.32	C Palace	29 Jun
16	Lee Bryan	Warks	200	823	22.90	Sheffield	12 Jul
17	Liam Walsh	Clwyd	DTB	823	45.88	Birmingham	17 Aug
18	Tyrone Keating	Essex	200	822	22.91	Sheffield	12 Jul
19	Mark Lewis-Francis	W Mids	100	819	11.37	Sheffield	12 Jul
20	Antony Flaherty	–	200	818	22.7	Ipswich	23 Jun

Women Under-15

Pos		County	Event	Points	Performance	Venue	Date
1	Fiona Harrison	S Yorks	PV	1013	3.50	Stoke	25 Aug
2	Sarah Zawada	Hants	200	987	24.6	Portsmouth	8 Jun
3	Helen Worsey	Leics	75HG	984	11.05w	Sheffield	13 Jul
4	Luisa Giles	Staffs	75HG	976	11.09w	Sheffield	13 Jul
5	Rachel Redmond	Staffs	100	972	12.21	Sheffield	12 Jul
6	Kimberly Canning	Scwest	200	970	25.07	Birmingham	18 Aug
7	Clare Russell	G Man	100	967	12.24	Sheffield	12 Jul
8	Emma Ward	Staffs	800	966	2:10.9	Solihull	30 Jun
9	Jenny Mockler	Mersey	1500	964	4:31.70	Cudworth	3 Aug
10	Erica Burfoot	S Glam	200	958	25.22	Swansea	6 Jul
11	Nikki Daniels	Staffs	800	955	2:11.6	Solihull	30 Jun
12	Louise O'Callaghan	London	75HG	952	11.43	Sheffield	12 Jul
13	Sharon Davidge	Devon	75HG	952	11.21w	Sheffield	13 Jul
14	Laura Watkins	Shrops	200	949	25.1	Brierley Hill	21 Jul
15	Rachel Harris	Mersey	HJ	948	1.72	Stoke	22 Jun
16	Sophie McQueen	Humber	HJ	948	1.72	Sheffield	12 Jul
17	Jenny McCarthy	Ches	200	945	25.39	Sheffield	12 Jul
18	Leah Tribe	Hants	200	945	25.39	Sheffield	12 Jul
19	Aimee Cutler	Gwent	200	941	25.45	Swansea	6 Jul
20	Melissa Anderson	Northumb	100	941	12.39	Sheffield	12 Jul

LAST ORDERS

Linford Christie bestrode athletics like a colossus for more than a decade until he retired from international athletics at the end of last season. PHIL MINSHULL, a regular contributor to the 'Daily Telegraph', pays tribute.

Overdrive: Stuttgart 93

TO ATHLETES and fans alike, this coming season will be a strange one. There will be no Linford Christ charging down the track across the world from Atlanta to Zurich.

Just when the Grand Old Man o global sprinting seemed destined to stay at the top for as long as Stanle Matthews, he has finally hung up his spikes.

No British athlete since the halcyon days of David Bedford has been able t fill stadiums like Christie and, although the next millennium has not yet been reached, there is no doubt that in any poll for the best British athlete of the last fifty years his only rivals would be Sebastian Coe and Daley Thompson

For honours and records the trio stand close comparison but only Christie has put his reputation on th line so often and against so many. The Jamaican-born sprinter seems to have been around for ever, and was an international runner for 15 years, but ironically he took a long time to make his mark on the sport.

Linford Christie's Gold Medals

1986	European Indoor Championships 200m
	European Championships 200m
1987	European Cup 100m
	European Cup 200m
1988	European Indoor Championships 60m
1989	European Cup 100m
	World Cup 100m
1990	European Indoor Championships 60m
	Commonwealth Games 100m
	European Championships 100m
1991	European Cup 200m
1992	Olympic Games 100m
	World Cup 100m
1993	European Cup 100m
	World Championships 100m
1994	European Championships 100m
	Commonwealth Games 100m
	European Cup 100m
	World Cup 100m
1995	European Cup 100m
	European Cup 200m
1996	European Cup 100m
	European Cup 200m

A man called Horse

On raw talent alone he came second in the 1979 English Schools 200m, and acquired the nickname 'Horse' from his London Schools team-mates because of his galloping gait. Perhaps Christie would have realised then he was destined for greatness if he had known that someone else had been given a similar monicker – the great Cuban thoroughbred Alberto Juantorena, who was known to his compatriots as 'El Caballo'.

Untutored at the time, soon afterwards he linked up with the unassuming Ron Roddan. An unlikely pair perhaps but Roddan became the coach who held sway over Christie's sprinting career thereafter.

Legend has it Christie was a far from assiduous pupil during their early association despite enjoying some modest success. His first international came indoors in 1981 against Germany, nevertheless his rare appearances at training led Roddan, in the spring of 1984, to threaten to stop coaching him.

The missive worked. The following year, at the age of 24, Christie made the European Indoor Championships in Athens, his first major championship. On that occasion he went out in the heats but next year he returned home from the same event in Madrid with the 200m title. The gold rush had started.

In June 1986 Christie supplanted Allan Wells as the fastest ever Briton, running 10.04 sec in the same Spanish city. That summer was completed with a European

FOR LINFORD

00m gold medal and a Commonwealth ames 100m silver medal, behind the rug-cheat Ben Johnson.

The following year saw further accolades. e became the first British athlete to win a uropean Cup sprint double and he shaved s British 100m record to 10.03 sec.

en-second barrier

y the summer of 1988 Christie was no nger just another good European printer but a man whom the previously ominant Americans started to fear. t the Seoul Olympics he took the 100m lver medal, behind Carl Lewis, and ecame the first European to break the n-second barrier with a time of 9.97 ec.

Into the bargain in Seoul he also otched up a British record of 20.09 sec the 200m final, a time that remains his est over the longer distance, although e just missed out on more honours hen finishing fourth.

By comparison, 1989 was a quiet year. hristie missed the World Indoor Champi- nships with a foot injury but bounced ack to win the European Cup and Vorld Cup 100m contests.

The former occasion was also notable or Christie being nominated to collect the up and in so doing he became the men's eam captain for the rest of his career.

The start of the 1990s saw Christie ack in full flight, retaining his European 00m title in Stuttgart and completing ome unfinished business by adding a ommonwealth 100m gold medal to his ollection.

Retirement...

Next year at the World Championships in okyo, Christie moved into another gear. He flew down the straight in a new uropean record 9.92 sec although, in what many still consider to be the best 00m final of all-time, he had to settle for ourth place behind an American clean weep lead by Lewis.

The relegation from the medal podium nitially caused dismay and he briefly con- emplated retiring. After all he was 31, and o other man had won the Olympic 00m title at his age. Nevertheless Christie at back and took stock of the situation nd decided that he still wanted to display is talents at the Olympics in Barcelona.

A season of single-minded concentra- on focused solely on just one point in me and just after 8pm on 1 August,

Power Pack: Barcelona 92

Christie shot out of his blocks posi- tioned in lane five of the Montjuic Stadium; 9.96 seconds later he joined the select band of men who can call themselves the fastest men in the world by virtue of having an Olympic gold medal to their name.

If Lewis and the rest were expecting Christie to rest on his laurels in 1993, they were very wrong. At the World Championships in Stuttgart he became the only man to simultaneously hold the quartet of World, Olympic, Commonwealth and European 100m titles with a thunderous run of 9.87 sec, just missing the much-sought world record by the smallest of margins.

The future

The question of when Linford will retire has been posed at the beginning of every recent season but the last three years hardly count as being the twilight of a career. In 1994 he retained his European and Commonwealth titles and, despite Leroy Burrell's new world record of 9.85 sec, he was the world's No 1 100m sprinter for the third year in a row.

Curate's eggs have nothing on Christie's 1995 year for being a mixture of good and bad. He set a 200m indoor world record of 20.25 sec in the French town of Lievin but later in the year, problems and disputes off the track got wide exposure and, nursing a leg injury, he had to settle for sixth in Gothenburg.

In Zurich though, he beat all the world's top men in a virtual repeat of the World Championship final and during the course of the season he beat Donovan Bailey, the new world cham- pion, five times out of nine encounters.

Which brings us to Christie's valedic- tory year. In June he notched up a record eleven individual European Cup wins and confounded the jeremiahs, who said it could not be done at the age of 36, by reaching the Olympic 100m final. Two false starts may not be the most satisfactory way to finish your last major championship final but when Christie looks back on his career the incident will only cause a brief gri- mace compared to all the memories which will generate a huge smile.

What now for Christie? We may not yet even have seen the last of the great man in a British vest. After what was supposed to be his final interna- tional appearance at Gateshead in August he hinted that he might yet be available to help Britain take on the European Cup holders Germany, in their own backyard in June.

'I will do it because it's in Munich and as a favour to my doctor,' said Christie, with reference to Hans-Muller Wolfhart who has cast his healing hands across Linford's limbs on many occasions. 'But that will be it. There will be no other international meetings.'

Regardless of his own future intentions he is already passing on his expertise to the next generation of British sprinters. Ian Mackie and Darren Campbell, young men who have both been dubbed by the media the next Linford Christie, have both been training with the great man in Australia recently.

Linford Christie has even outshone his contemporary Kenneth Branagh who produced his biography at a prodigious early age. But Christie already has two to his name.

And his influence has also extended far beyond athletics. David Coulthard recently described him as his inspiration. 'When you think about it, the 100m is over so quickly there is no time for the slightest flaw in technique or tempera- ment, so for Linford to have won as many important races as he has underlines his excellence,' said the Scottish Formula One racing driver. That last word from Coulthard – excellence – will be one for- ever associated with Christie.

'QUOTE......

'It's a rarity to get in a tactical race without Kenyans tearing about' – JOHN NUTTALL after winning the AAA 5000m title in June

'If I'm there, you will see me. If not, you won't' – LINFORD CHRISTIE, speaking in May and trying to keep everyone guessing about his Atlanta plans

'If this was anywhere else but America, I would have been allowed to run' – CHRISTIE after his disqualification following two false starts in the Olympic 100m final

'We've been married for three years but for two of those our lives have been dogged with pain. We're tired. We've had enough' – DIANE MODAHL, on her life with Vicente and being dubbed a drugs cheat

'It was a special day. I felt as nervous as I did at my first international' – JUDY OAKES, on her record seventy third international appearance for Great Britain, indoors in January

'Roger won't be holding the record for long. It's nothing personal because Roger is a nice chap but I'm going to turn the heat up more' – DU'AINE LADEJO, just before making his £1000 losing bet with Black (right) on just who would hold the British 400m record at the end of the season

'When I said I wasn't going to go to Atlanta, I meant it. But I changed my mind' – CHRISTIE, (below) announcing his change of heart in July

'After I win gold in Atlanta, there will still be a long way to go. After all, I'm not the world record holder' – DONOVAN BAILEY, tempting fate in January

'I didn't think a British record was on the cards. I didn't think we would have to run that fast' – ROGER BLACK, underestimating the domestic competition at 400m after winning the Olympic Trial in Birmingham

'At the time of the Olympic Games, this will be the safest city in the world' – Atlanta Organising Committee chief executive, BILLY PAYNE, speaking two months before the Games

'We plan to organise the best Games in history' – PAYNE, getting it wrong .... again

'There's just 100 days to go before the Olympic Games in Augusta' – BBC commentator DAVID COLEMAN, with just enough time for a geography lesson

UNQUOTE '

'When I retired in 1992, I'd had a bellyful of track and field. Nothing was going to get me back' – TESSA SANDERSON, looking fabulous at 40, on the day she returned to competition at a wet and windy Bedford

'When I think about the events of 1984, it's a bit like reading a novel about someone else. Am I happy now? Just about' – ZOLA BUDD, speaking in Majorca at the World Half-Marathon Championships in September

'My wife was watching the race on TV but I told her, if I ran well, to get on the first train and meet me at the hotel. She got on the 12 o'clock from Lowestoft, so she'll arrive tomorrow' – PAUL EVANS, on making family connections after finishing third in April's Flora London Marathon

'Marathon running is a different sport, it's not normal running. I must have a screw loose. I can't believe I want to put myself through it again' – GARY STAINES, ninth in London, and telling it like it is

'I noticed a blue blur and a swoosh. When Johnson went past me on the turn, I thought, "Oh well, there goes first"' – Trinidad's ATO BOLDON, on trying to cope with Johnson's 19.32 in Atlanta

'I was born with a love for athletics. I can't help myself. I should probably stop all this and get a proper job' – The mercurial JON RIDGEON, on being fit, healthy and back in the big-time

'I don't give no free rent upstairs. You have to earn your spot in this brain' – CARL LEWIS, (above) speaking in March, on how he deals with his critics

'Michael and I sat together after the race and he was saying, "I can't believe it, I can't believe it". I said, "You're joking, aren't you?"' – BLACK, incredulous after his Olympic 400m silver medal behind that man Johnson again

'I could lose horribly but it's not everything. The most important thing in my life is my relationship with God and that remains unaffected' – JONATHAN EDWARDS, on the eve of the Olympic triple jump competition

'I wanted to make history and now I'm afraid of what I might be able to run' – MICHAEL JOHNSON after his Olympic 200m gold medal in a world record time

'I'll be behind the scenes. You won't see me pushing myself to the forefront and talking about these guys' – CHRISTIE on retirement and his new role as coach to protégés, Ian Mackie and Darren Campbell

'To say I'm disappointed must be the understatement of the year' – Ireland's SONIA O'SUL-LIVAN after failing to finish the Olympic 5000m final

'After Atlanta, I thought, "I've had enough. I'm going to have babies." But Jon talked me out of it' – SALLY GUNNELL, reflecting on how life might have been different in retirement until her husband intervened

Sport for Shelter

Are you attending sporting events throughout the year? Are you a runner, walker or maybe you fancy jumping out of a plane at 10,000 feet or bungee jumping? If so, why not consider raising money for Shelter at the same time?

Shelter is the largest, most established charity helping homeless and badly housed people and the only national one. Unique in the provision of practical help and advice as well as campaigning for long term change to tackle the problems of homelessness and poor housing.

Last year we helped over 100,000 people through our network of 50 Housing Aid Centres and projects countrywide whose caseworkers give free, impartial, professional legal and practical advice to those in housing need. Although rough sleeping is the most visible and severe form of homelessness many more households, including families with children, the elderly and vulnerable live in appalling conditions of squalor, overcrowding and insecurity; conditions which are totally unacceptable.

"I came to Shelter for help after I got into arrears following my husband's death. The building society wanted to repossess the house which has been my home for the last 25 years.

Shelter dealt with the building society, bank and solicitors. Shelter's help resulted in the building society agreeing to a monthly repayment I can afford and long term security. My family, and me especially, can't praise Shelter enough for all its done."

Shelter relies on the continued support of people like yourself to run its vital services. Total expenditure on the direct charitable objectives of housing aid services and communications in 1995/6 was £8.9 million and continues to rise with new projects and initiatives.

So run, walk, swim, jump.....for Shelter! Make a real difference to the lives of homeless and badly housed people around the country. For further information call 0171 505 2075.

Shelter

Registered Charity Number 263710
Registered Company Number 1038133

PART TWO

FOCUS ON THE WORLD CHAMPIONSHIPS

BRITISH SUCCESS AT THE WORLD CHAMPIONSHIPS

British athletes have provided the five previous IAAF World Championships with many of their truly magical moments.

HELSINKI

At the first ever Championships, in Helsinki in 1983, it was the emergence of Steve Cram which lifted the spirits after a week of so many near gold medal misses. Already the European and Commonwealth champion from 1982 – when messrs Coe and

STEVE CRAM

Ovett were absent injured – Cram faced his first real test at world level in Finland. In a scrappy final in which both Ovett and Said Aouita made crucial tactical errors, the 22–year-old Cram emerged the victor.

The second gold medal of a Championships still regarded as the best by many observers, came from the master of the decathlon, Daley Thompson, who confirmed his status as the world's greatest ever all-rounder.

Those Championships will also be remembered for Peter Elliott's fourth place after a typically gutsy front run in the 800m and for the smile which lit up Colin Reitz's face as he was gifted a bronze medal in the steeplechase. There were tears for Fatima Whitbread as she lost out on gold only when Finnish heroine Tiina Lillak produced a winning final throw in the javelin. Kathy Cook won a bronze medal behind Marita Koch and Merlene Ottey in the 200m and the men's 400m relay team began its medal winning run with third place behind the Soviet Union.

FATIMA WHITBREAD

ROME

Rome, in the summer of 1987, belonged to Fatima Whitbread when she won Britain's only gold medal of the second Championships. There should have been another gold though. John Regis will forever agonise over the way he dipped too soon in the 200m. The mistake lost him two places but, at just 20, he won a glorious bronze medal nevertheless. Two other 20-year-olds, high hurdlers Jon Ridgeon and Colin Jackson ushed defending champion [G]reg Foster all the way to the [li]ne to earn silver and bronze. [Ja]ck Buckner followed up his [E]uropean success with third [p]lace behind Aouita in the [5]000m and the 4x400m relay [s]quad took silver behind the [A]mericans. Five years after the [e]vent the IAAF disqualified Ben [J]ohnson as 100m champion [a]fter he admitted taking drugs [a]nd the decision meant that [L]inford Christie was elevated [fr]om fourth to third in the offi[c]ial results. There were disap[p]ointments too. The champi[o]nship marked the end of Steve [C]ram's reign as the world No1 [o]ver 1500m. He finished eighth.

TOKYO

[F]ive athletes and two gold [m]edals took the headlines in [T]okyo fours later. Liz [M]cColgan ran the finest race of

her career to win the 10,000m while the 400m relay quartet of Roger Black, Derek Redmond, John Regis and Kriss Akabusi scored a famous victory over the Americans in the final event of the Championships. Black had earlier won a silver medal in the individual 400m, Akabusi a bronze in the 400mh, in his first season at the event. Sally Gunnell also won silver in the women's 400mh. Tony Jarrett took bronze in a 110mh final missing the injured Colin Jackson. Britain's sprint relay foursome of Jarrett, Regis, Darren Braithwaite and Christie finished third behind the Americans' world record.

Z McCOLGAN

SALLY GUNNELL

STUTTGART

Christie, Jackson and Gunnell had reached the peak of their careers by the time the Championships became biennial and arrived in Stuttgart in 1993. Christie, now the Olympic champion, came agonisingly close to the world record in winning the 100m while

COLIN JACKSON

Gunnell – also Olympic champion – went one better in the 400mh, beating Sandra Farmer-Patrick in a classic encounter in a new world record of 52.74. Jackson, fighting off the demons which had plagued his Olympic campaign, scored his greatest ever victory in the 110mh in 12.91, a new world record. Jarrett claimed an English record and the silver medal with 13.00.

Regis finished the Championships with two silver medals; one for the 200m and another as part of the 4x100m team which also included Jackson, Jarrett and Christie. In what became Britain's best ever World Championships, there was success in the field too. Steve Smith (high jump), Mike Hill (javelin) and Jonathan Edwards (triple jump) all won bronze medals.

GOTHENBURG

Despite his bronze medal in Stuttgart, Jonathan Edwards could not have forseen the events of 1995. No other athlete in history could have done so much right in a single season. In the World Championship triple jump final in Gothenburg, he twice bettered his own world record in successive jumps – the first time the feat had ever been achieved – and won the gold medal by the biggest ever margin seen in World Championship and Olympic history since 1896. His was the only gold of the Championships but Kelly Holmes came close to a magnificent double in the 800m and 1500m. She ended with bronze and silver medals. There were also silver medals for Jarrett (110mh), Steve Backley (javelin) and notable performances from Smith (fourth in the high jump), Peter Whitehead (fourth in the marathon) and Mark Richardson (fifth in the 400m).

JONATHAN EDWARDS

BY TOM KNIGHT

ATHENS AND THE SIXTH IAAF WORLD CHAMPIONSHIPS

Following the debacle of Atlanta, it is fitting that the sixth IAAF World Championships are in Athens, the city which should have hosted the Centennial Olympics.

The Championships will be the biggest sporting event to be held in Greece since the first of the Modern Olympics in 1896. Athens' timing could not have been better. The Championships, from 1–10 August, take place on the eve of the IOC's final selection of cities bidding to host the 2004 Olympics. It is inconceivable that the city will again miss out on the chance to host the Games.

The Greeks – who have a passionate interest in sport – are no strangers to major athletics events. The 1982 European Championships, the 1985 European Indoor Championships, the first World Junior Championships, the 1990 IAAF Grand Prix Final, the 1991 Mediterranean Games and the 1995 World Marathon Cup have all been staged in Athens.

In the beginning

It is to the Greeks that we must look for the first evidence of athletics organised on a grand scale. Homer's *Illiad* describes the sports of running, jumping, throwing, wrestling and boxing at the Funeral Games for Patroclus in around 800 BC. Up until 776 BC the Olympics had been mainly a religious festival in honour of Zeus, followed by the *dromos*, a sprint along the length of the stadium measured at about 192 yards. When the Games became a sporting event, distance races were introduced along with jumps, discus and javelin competitions and a pentathlon. Chariot races, music and poetry competitions were also featured. The Olympics were permanently based at Olympia, Ellis, a small province in southern Greece and held every four years. Such was their importance that all battles were suspended for the five days of competition.

Even then, champions were hailed as heroes, rewarded well and afforded all manner of priviliges. The prize may have been just a crown of garlands but winners knew that life after an Olympic win would never be quite the same again. The first ever association of 'professional' athletes was formed around 50 BC.

The Games' eventual decline reflected in many ways the decline of the ancient Greek civilisation. Greece lost its independence to Rome in the middle of the second century and the Games were finally abolished by the Roman Emperor Theodosius in AD 393, not to be revived until 1896.

Acknowledging the past

The 1997 World Championships will acknowledge those Games by staging the men's and women's marathons on the ancient course from Marathon to the 80,000 capacity Panathinaikon Marble Stadium in the centre of Athens. This is the very stadium in which Spiros Louis, the first champion of the event, entered as winner of the first modern Olympic Games in 1896. It will be the first time in the history of the World Championships that the start and finish of the marathons will not be held at the stadium that will host all the other events. The men's marathon will be held on Saturday, 9 August and the women's race on Sunday, 10 August (both starting at 8am).

The rest of the events will be staged in Athens' Olympic Stadium which seats 75,000 spectators. The stadium was first used for the 1982 European Championships and will be the centre-piece of the city's bid for the 2004 Olympics.

Modern champions already have their lives changed by success in the sporting arena but this year, for the first time, the IAAF has introduced prize money at its world championships. In Athens, gold medallists will receive $60,000, silver medallists $30,000 and bronze medallists $20,000 though they shouldn't rule out a crown of garlands to go with the cheques.

Towards the future

Only too aware of the negative vibes which affected its bid for the Centennial Olympics, Athens has worked hard to improve its image in recent years. The city's notorious environmental problems are gradually being reduced and Athens has undergone a major facelift in the last five years. Air quality has improved and work is

ATHENS OLYMPIC STADIUM ...Venue for the 1997 World Championships

well under way on revamping the airport and Metro system. Most of this work, however, is scheduled for completion in line with the Olympic bid.

The well-documented problem of traffic does still exist. Despite the fact that August is the month when Athenians traditionally take their holidays, there will inevitably be congestion in the busy city centre streets. The heat and humidity could add to the frustration of athletes, media and spectators travelling to the stadium.

Making the Championships as hassle-free as possible will, of course, be uppermost in the organising committee's planning. There is too much at stake for this major sporting event to be anything less than successful. Internal disagreements have now been resolved and IAAF President, Dr Primo Nebiolo has already suggested that this will be the greatest World Championships ever held. After Atlanta, we will all look forward to that.

SAY ALOE TO VERA AND ALL HER MATES!

There has been a great deal of press comment over the past eighteen months or so about the many and varied benefits of aloe vera as the "miracle cure" for the 21st Century.

But aloe vera isn't just a modern phenomena, it has been noted for its potent healing qualities for centuries. Greek physicians such as Dioscorides and Pliny used aloe extensively, and it has even been suggested that athletes at the original Olympic games over two thousand years ago used it to boost energy levels.

Aloe vera is now available for everyone to use, both internally and externally, either as a pure natural product or mixed with a variety of other exotic ingredients such as royal jelly or shea nut butter. Many of these are for external use as creams, gels or lotions to assist with skin repair and rejuvenation, but, at long last a drink is available combining the many benefits of aloe vera with some other exciting and quite remarkable natural products.

These include evening primrose oil a plant with almost as many healing properties as aloe vera, and Eleutherococcus Senticosus, sometimes also known as "Siberian Ginseng", a substance which is officially recommended by the Russian Ministry of Sport for all Russian athletes as well as being used by Cosmonauts to counter space sickness.

This exceptional drink, produced exclusively by Beck's Aloe Co. has a refreshing mixed-fruit flavour, provides a daily dose of each of the prime ingredients in a handy bottle, yet has only one calorie per serving.

Beck's new "Elixir of Life" drink should be taken whenever you undergo a period of special stress or need to adapt to new circumstances. It may also be taken to counteract the effects of severe physical training, or during convalesence after illness or injury. The three major ingredients also have very strong detoxification properties, which assist the body remove harmful substances, including excess alcohol.

To find out more about aloe vera, evening primrose oil and "Siberian Ginseng" send a stamped addressed envelope to Beck's Aloe Co. PO Box 4, Chislehurst, Kent, BR7 5TG.

From the early days of sport, athletes have been looking for new ways of improving their performance. With the rapid advances in technology, it has been possible for innovative physiologists to discover routes to better performance. Passing this information on to the coaches to disseminate to the athletes, has meant more work.

Two facts about fitness are true. One, heart rate monitoring in training improves performance. Secondly, heart rate monitors are improving with technology, to be more reliable and advanced in features. This means, that all athletes should use a monitor, but they should also be able to use and understand it, to suit the programme they have worked out with their coach.

PulseTronic have taken the technology of heart rate monitoring. They have made it not only reliable, but also easy to understand. The range of PulseTronic monitors are all affordable and cover most of the features, the average athlete would be looking for. The British Biathlon Union selected PulseTronic as the official supplier because in the cold winter training sessions they did not want to place stress on the athlete. No matter what the sport, from triathlon to cycling and athletics, international level athletes have chosen to use PulseTronic heart rate monitors, because they are easy to use and have sensible features.

When putting together an endurance programme - Frequency - Intensity - and Time - are the main three factors. A good programme and training diary can log frequency. Intensity can best be controlled through heart rate monitoring, especially with upper and lower limit functions on the monitor. Ideally with lactate threshold work-outs setting should be as accurate as one beat. Time spent training should also be monitored by the athlete. All these functions are available for as little as £69.99 this summer with the introduction of the Blitz monitor.

The memory function on the PulseLink will record time spend above, in or below training zone to show the amount of quality time in a given work-out. Both the PulseLink and Vanguard incorporate recovery pulse, which would help monitor improvement in heart/lung performance.

Research amongst heart rate monitor users shows, that the coach regularly uses advanced features. However, owners universally use heart rate and stopwatch functions. They sometimes use training zones and apart from a backlight and looking at the time of day, they use the other features less than once a month. With the large use being at the lower end of the market PulseTronic monitors now make practical heart rate monitoring affordable for the majority of users. *For more information contact IDASS Fitness, sole UK agent for PulseTronic in the UK on 01753-790330.*

Get involved! - help Shaftesbury support people facing disability or poverty

David Davies, who lives in a house owned by Shaftesbury in Halifax, has proved that having a learning difficulty is no obstacle to athletic achievement. David came third out of 26 runners in the Yorkshire and Humberside championship in March 1996, and since then has gained a place in the national team. He has also won a silver in the 800 and 1,500 metre races in the 10 Nation International Meeting. His coach has high hopes for David, and he has entered other competitions including the Mini-Olympics in Hull in August last year.

For more information about any aspect of our work, please contact us at this address:

150 years of Christian care in action

The Shaftesbury Society,
16 Kingston Road, London SW19 1JZ
Tel. 0181 239 5555 Fax: 0181 239 5580

Registered in England number 38751.   Registered Charity number 221948

ABOUT SHAFTESBURY

The Shaftesbury Society's roots are in the Seventh Earl of Shaftesbury's Ragged Schools Union, supported by Charles Dickens and where Dr. Barnardo and General Gordon both taught.

Today Shaftesbury are one of the country's leading providers of care and education services to people with learning and/or physical disabilities, as well as still providing support and development services to people who are poor or disadvantaged.

Shaftsbury exits to enable people in great need to achieve security, self-worth and significance and through this to show Christian care in action.

Shaftesbury shows Christian care in action through:

- Care and education services for **people with a disability**
- Hostels and resettlement services for **people who are homeless**
- Day care services for **older people**
- Affordable furniture, advice, employment training and more for **people on low incomes**
- And **helping churches** respond to local community needs

So Good, They Did it Twice

With their golden doubles in Atlanta Michael Johnson and Marie-Jose Perec became two of the greatest Olympians in history. TOM KNIGHT and NICOLA DAVIES discover that the future holds the same target for the two superstars

HISTORY MAKER . . . Johnson celebrates

THAT great sage, Roger Black, perhaps best summed up the phenomenon that is Michael Johnson when he highlighted the difference between the American and the rest of the world's best 400m runners.

'Michael's in a class of his own,' he said. 'He could run with two fingers stuck up his bottom and still beat the rest of us.'

The point was never better illustrated than at last summer's Olympics when Johnson delivered what he had been threatening all year – glorious gold medals in the individual 400m - in which Black took silver – and the 200m, where he produced the performance of the Games to beat Frankie Fredericks and slashed more than three-tenths of a second off his own six-week-old world record in clocking 19.32.

It was not just the Americans who wanted Johnson to achieve the historic 200/400m double. The International Amateur Athletic Federation quite liked the idea too. It even altered the track and field timetable so that the sport's biggest name could achieve the same feat he had achieved at the 1995 World Championships.

Pitter-patter style
Johnson, the son of a truck driver wit the upright stance and pitter-patter running style duly obliged by making winning eight races in six days look a too easy. He had at last erased the bad memories of four years earlier when he had failed so dramatically to win the 200m in Barcelona. Food poi soning was the cause that time. In Atlanta he had left nothing to chance and his races were dispatched with the cool deliberation that has become his trade mark.

It was Fredericks who provided the only interruption to Johnson's magnificent season, ending his 38-race winning streak by beating him in a closely fought 200m in Oslo in early July. It wa thought then that with Johnson's aura of invincibility shattered, his Olympic dream was in doubt. But, in the Centennial Olympic Stadium a month later, the Namibian had no answer to Johnson's blistering acceleration off the

AWESOME . . . Michael Johnson (left) and in action during the 200m was the athlete of the Games.

end on a day when everything went right for the athlete dubbed Superman. slo was forgotten in an instant.

The 400m final had been no differnt, with Black left ten yards adrift as ohnson surged through the line in 3.49, a new Olympic record but still vo-tenths of a second short of Butch eynolds' eight-year-old world mark.

With now World and Olympic titles both distances and after six years of rinting supremacy, Johnson's remaing target is that 400m world record. ow 29, the accounting and marketg graduate from Texas, with sponsornip contracts alone worth a reputed 1 million a year, will go into the 1997 ason with his reputation once more the line.

The world championships in Athens eckon and, if the weather is right, e opposition is ready to take him on nd if Johnson himself is in prime contion, there appears no earthly reason hy the man cannot claim the world cord that has, somehow, always emed rightfully his.

The flickering screen holds the key. With ore and more sports locked in a holy war capture hearts and minds, athletics eeds idols with telegenic charm. Beautiful inners are worth their weight in gold.

TYLISH . . . Marie Jose Perec is just at home on e catwalk.

ON THE LINE . . . Marie-Jose Perec beats Marlene Othey (left) in the 200m to complete her double.

And Marie-Jose Perec knows all about gold. She won her first World Championship title at 400m in 1991, her second in 1995. She was Olympic 400m champion in 1992, the first person in history to retain an Olympic 400m title in Atlanta and only the second to achieve the 200m/400m double – 15 minutes before another MJ.

Only a career-capping world record has been elusive. Perec had often said that the 400m world record of 47.60 set by Marita Koch in 1985 was an impossible, dream-like mark. But after running 48.25 in Atlanta – the fastest time in the world for ten years – she has changed her mind.

'There are certain conditions: I need to be in the best shape, I need a fast track, a crowd like Zurich's ... and I need Gwen Torrence,' Perec said. 'Remember, in Atlanta I ran 48.25 one day after running 49.19...'

France's greatest sportswoman, born in the Caribbean island of Guadaloupe, only came to Paris when she was 16 and then moved to the USA in 1994. This was partly to escape the ferocious attention that comes with celebrity and partly to find a new coach in John Smith after her relationship with Jacques Piasenta, the man who helped her win Olympic gold in 1992, turned sour.

Doing homework

By taking up the challenge of a new country, an alien culture and language, she has found her real home and the space she needed to come to terms with life. Intent on leading as normal a life as possible Perec fills the little spare time she has at home in Beverly Hills by going to the movies, painting and helping her 11-year-old nephew with his homework when he comes to stay.

The extraordinary coverage Perec got in the French media before and after the Games showed why her quest for a quiet life took her abroad. Understandably, she was on the cover of every sports magazine but she also made the cover of Elle, Paris Match, VSD and five other national magazines.

In the July edition of Elle, the sprinter occupied half the contents. There was an interview, a feature of Perec's birthplace of Guadaloupe, beauty tips and even her recipes! But best of all was a stunning photo spread shot in Death Valley showing Perec in a selection of haute couture dresses. 'I love fashion,' she said. 'I love doing model shots.'

Perec has an elegance that makes her remarkable athletic achievements seem all the sweeter. Any athlete as tall, pretty, and long-legged as Perec has a genetic advantage of course. And fortunately, Perec's running style makes no attempt to mess with nature. She does not really look fast, she looks cool and she crosses the line first. Take a bow Marie-Jose.

CARRYING ON THE TRADITION

He did not qualify for the Olympics last year but Daniel Komen still ended up as the best distance runner in the world. Here, we look back on an incredible year for the Kenyan who is set to rule the world into the next millennium

THE PUPIL AND HIS MASTER . . . Daniel Komen (top) is coached by Moses Kiptanui

A KENYAN athlete lopes majestically through the bush, his training run carrying him towards another world record-breaking attempt. Daniel Komen, from the 8000ft high village of Nyaru, north-west of Nairobi, seems happily at home, although the habitat is not the Rift Valley, but England's Thames Valley.

A whole tribe of Kenyans can be found training around Teddington during the European Grand Prix season. They stay in houses rented by their agent, Kim McDonald, whose huge stable of runners from the Dark Continent suggests he is the sport's Dr Livingstone.

Sometimes there are up to 30 Kenyan athletes in residence down by the riverside close to Richmond Park, where Sebastian Coe often still runs, which they see as a suitable training environment for Heathrow Airport and the European circuit.

Lean patch

For Britain, going through an unaccustomed lean patch in middle-distance running, there is at least some consolation that this south-west London suburb is their second home. Just a few miles from the Harrow fields on which, two generations ago, Roger Bannister ran before becoming the first sub-four-

minute miler, the twenty-year-old Komen runs today: a man with the capacity to run two sub-four-minute miles, back-to-back, with no rest.

In the Italian seaside resort of Rieti last September that was virtually what he did. Frustrated by having had to watch the Olympics on TV because he failed to qualify for the Kenyan team, he poured his pent-up energies into setting a world 3000 metres record of 7:20.67 – seven-and-a-half laps at an average of 58.76secs. According to *Track & Field News*, the time equates to 7:55.92 for the full two miles; back-to-back miles averaging 3:57.96. Incredible.

It was the culmination of an amazing post-Olympic campaign by Komen. The rest of the world's athletes, still recovering from Atlanta, were left astonished by his performances. None more so than the Ethiopian Haile Gebresilasie, the 10,000m gold medallist and world 5000m record holder, who Komen destroyed with a display of sustained front-running not seen at this level since Steve Ovett forced John Walker to step off the track during the 1500m at the 1977 World Cup. For once, the clock hardly mattered but when Komen hit the tape his time of 12:45.09 was just 0.70 outside Gebresilasie's world record.

Firepower

Noureddine Morceli, the Olympic 1500m champion, was the next to feel the youngster's firepower, losing his first race for two years when he finished behind him over 3000m in Brussels. Then victory in the 5000m over the Moroccan Salah Hissou, the new world 10,000m record holder, at the IAAF Grand Prix final in Milan clinched Komen the overall title and the biggest cheque in track and field history – $250,000.

While so many athletes were relying on Atlanta for their meal ticket to the future, the man who missed it all has done better than most. One estimate is that his purple patch will have earned him around $400,000 in a month. The income has set Komen up for life and enabled his mother to give up her job selling potatoes by the roadside.

No one could accuse the success of going to his head, though. 'It was a nice way to end the season but I think I still have room for improvement before I am a good runner,' said Komen, a modest young man with a polite manner. He does not insist on the superstar treatment so many American and European athletes now demand from meeting organisers.

When he joined McDonald and his Kenyan colleagues for the IAAF's trip to

MOSES AND THE PROMISED LAND ...
Kiptanui leading, predicts great things for Komen

avajero for the Solidarity Meeting, the day after his victory in Milan, he stood atiently by the roadside as he waited for a us in Bosnia, and when the vehicle finally rrived insisted that a group of British ournalists board it before him. 'You look old,' he said to them. And even when the us splashed him with a puddle as it ulled away he did not complain.

Komen's post-Atlanta record-breaking pree mirrors that of the man who has aken him under his wing, and now dvises him, enjoyed four years ago. Moses Kiptanui broke two world records n three days after missing Barcelona with knee injury. 'I'm very happy for Daniel,' aid Kiptanui. 'He can run under 12:50 or 5000m next year.'

Awesome potential

McDonald, who also helps Komen work ut his training, is also convinced of his lient's awesome potential. 'I think he ould ultimately have a range between 3:32 [for 1500m] and 26:30 [for 10,000m],' aid the Englishman who in his time has vorked with some of the world's greatest distance runners, including Ovett, Grete Waitz and Liz McColgan.

Komen failed to make Kenya's Atlanta team not because he was injured ut simply because he finished outside he first three in the sudden-death trial.

Having also missed out on the 1995 World Championships in Gothenburg, it was particularly disappointing. He is at a loss to explain the reason, but both him and McDonald believe it may be because he performs better at sea-level than altitude. Yet the 13:29.33 he ran in Nairobi in 1994 broke John Ngugi's world altitude record by more than a second. It seems hard to believe that Komen will not qualify for this year's IAAF World Championships in Athens and start winning the medals his talent really deserves.

Komen has been earmarked as a future world-beater ever since finishing second in the junior race at the World Cross Country Championships in 1993 and the following year won the 5000/ 10,000m double at the World Junior Championships in Lisbon, when he succeeded Gebresilasie as champion in both.

Those performances also came off the back of a setback. 'I should have gone to the World Junior Championships in Seoul in 1992,' Komen explained. 'But I was 16 and inexperienced and I was removed from the team. I was very disappointed but I went home to prove that I was a good runner.'

He started doing that when he pushed Kiptanui to the world 5000m record in Rome last year. Komen was leading coming into the home straight

but Kiptanui surged past to win in 12:55.30 with Komen second in 12:56.15, also inside Gebresilasie's then world record of 12:56.96. 'That record belonged as much to Daniel as me,' said Kiptanui. 'Without him I could never have broken it. It was then that people appreciated how great a runner he had the potential to be.'

Fearless

Watching Komen in action it is clear that he runs without fear. He thinks anything and everything is possible. 'The young ones are training with world champions and they feel it is natural that they will be as good as them,' explained Kiptanui, the self-appointed guardian for the next generation of great African runners. 'Kenyans don't set limits like the Europeans and Americans.'

Komen was brought up in the Rift Valley where there is no public transport and few people own cars. He saw the likes of Kiptanui, and what running has brought him, and decided to dedicate himself to getting some of that for himself. 'Because of the economic rewards available Kenyan runners are prepared to work very hard,' Kiptanui said.

Inevitably, the burn-out rate is high among the Kenyans. They run too fast and too often, frequently breaking records five years ahead of their time. Theirs can be a butterfly existence but under the guidance of wise old head Kiptanui and the canny Yorkshireman McDonald you get the feeling that young Master Komen may be around for a few years to come yet. Sit back and enjoy it.

STEP UP
THE PACE

We have all suffered from foot problems at some time in our lives and if you consider that an active person will take over 18,000 steps a day, it is hardly surprising that feet sometimes object loudly to their treatment!

An array of foot conditions are commonly found in adults who lead busy active lives, in particular the 25-50 age group.

*t*ACKLE
ATHLETE'S FOOT

Athlete's foot is a rival your feet can live without - but it's often on the rampage in changing rooms and communal bathing areas, like swimming pools and showers. Keep this highly contagious fungal infection out of the game with Scholl's new look range of Athlete's Foot products comprising a spray, cream and powder.

The range contains tolnaftate which destroys the Athlete's Foot fungi that causes the infection relieving the itching and soreness and preventing reinfection.
*always read the label

*b*EAT
FOOT ODOUR

Competition may come from a challenging rival - foot odour! With your feet containing around 250.000 sweat glands - more sweat glands than any other part of your body, this is hardly surprising. Scholl's new look active Odour Control range is ideal for helping sports enthusiasts to treat and help prevent serious foot odour and wetness, For a winning result, beat foot odour for good with Super Odour Control insoles Inserted into your sports shoes. These are the most effective odour fighting insoles available, containing an activated charcoal layer to absorb and neutralise the odour, they also contain an antibacterial agent to destroy the cause of foot odour and help prevent reoccurrence.

Scholl's Odour Control range also includes a selection of sprays, powder and a cream. And new in 1996 an improved extra-strength formulation for Odour Control Foot Spray.

Offering 24 hour protection. It contains both deodorant and anti-perspirant ingredients to stop odour and wetness and keep feet fresh and odour-free.

SCHOLL and the SCHOLL logo are registered trademarks

*t*IP
TOP TOES

footcare

You don't have to be one of the nine out of 10 who suffer from these or many other foot problems - a little forward thinking can prevent foot problems and make an enormous contribution to your overall sporting performance. Exercise can help considerably to keep your feet healthy. Exercise tones up weakened muscles and helps to strengthen fallen arches which may be causing discomfort.

A simple five-point footcare plan can also help to get feet into good shape and keep them that way. Follow the plan regularly for attractive, cool and comfortable feet.

*   *1 Bathe and dry feet* Begin by bathing feet for 10 minutes in warm water and Scholl Soothing Foot Bath to relax and soothe them.
*   *2 Trim nails straight across* Never cut or file down the sides of nails as this can lead to ingrown toenails.
*   *3 Remove rough skin* To ensure smooth, comfortable feet, remove rough dry skin by using a foot file or rough skin remover-such as Scholl Exfoliating Foot Cream - to leave feet feeling soft and smooth.
*   *4 Tone up* Moisturise and tone feet by massaging them with a foot lotion or cream, for example Scholl Softening Lotion or Scholl Deep Moisturising Cream.
*   *5 Refresh* To complete the treatment, use an invigorating Scholl Refreshing Foot Spray or Scholl Cooling Foot Powder - to ensure feet remain fragrant and comfortably cool.

*f*OR A
BLISTERING PERFORMANCE

blisters

Blisters are all too common a problem for sporting enthusiasts, so remember them and how painful they can be if you don't have the right treatment available. Blisters are an extremely common problem - recent research shows that 5.2 million people suffer from them each year but very few of us know what to do.

Scholl races forward to the rescue of all those suffering from blisters, be it from new sports shoes, a racquet, or simply overdoing it on the running machine in the gym.

Keep Scholl Blister Treatment in your sports bag - it is specially designed to help give rapid relief from blisters - when an ordinary plaster will only conceal your blister, this treatment has a hydrocolloid dressing which soothes and promotes rapid healing, giving immediate pain relief for unhappy toes and feet! Whilst the strong hypoallergenic adhesive will ensure it stays in place while you carry on playing.

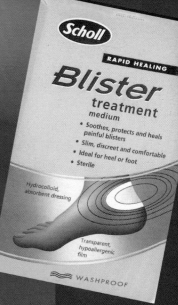

Scholl

RAPID HEALING

Blister
treatment
medium

*   Soothes, protects and heals painful blisters
*   Slim, discreet and comfortable
*   Ideal for heel or foot
*   Sterile

Hydrocolloid, absorbent dressing

Transparent, hypoallergenic film

WASHPROOF

LEWIS NEARS THE FINISH TAPE . . .

IF THERE were any doubts about Carl Lewis's claim to the title of the greatest athlete of all time, then his outstanding performance to take a fourth Olympic long jump gold in Atlanta effectively ended the argument.

Already sure of his place in history, Lewis emerged from the Games as one of only two men – the other being discus thrower Al Oerter – to win four consecutive golds in the same athletics event. His overall tally of nine golds also equalled the record of the legendary Finn, Paavo Nurmi.

With an audacious piece of theatre typical of the man, Lewis exceeded even his own expectations to snatch a victory in Atlanta which was made still more dramatic by his near-elimination at the qualifying stage. On the same day that Michael Johnson won the 400m on the way to his historic double, the grand old man of track and field came damn close to pinching all the headlines.

Dream maker

All but written off before the Olympics, Lewis didn't just come back in Atlanta; he soared across the arena having galvanised all the speed, grace and heart he could muster from a career that had seen him win eight gold medals at previous Games in Los Angeles, Seoul and Barcelona. Lewis, the dream maker, knew he had to produce something special to win a gold medal this time around. He did.

His record-equalling win at the age of 35 came, essentially, with two jumps. The first, of 8.29m, saw him qualify for

Hollywood Glory: Lewis wins the 100m in LA '84

the final with the last of his three attempts. The second, of 8.50m, in the third round of the final, was simply too good for the rest. It was vintage stuff. And this after he had only scraped into the American team with a less than impressive display at the US trials six weeks earlier. 'This is the biggest moment of my entire career,' he said afterwards. 'There's no way I can top this.' How many times must he have thought that in a career like his?

But then, Lewis has always been quality personified, the supreme competitor. He always told us never to write him off, even long after everyone had. On the biggest stage of all, he proved yet again that he was right and we were wrong.

There was no finer sight in athletics than that of Lewis, in full flow and sweeping past the world's best sprinters in a 100m race. In Los Angeles in 1984, he equalled Jesse Owens's feat of winning four Olympic golds, set two world records at 100m – including the 9.86 sec with which he astonished the world in Tokyo in 1991 – ran the most sub-10 sec 100m and recorded the most 28ft long jumps.

World icon

He was, too, the first superstar of the modern era, commanding fees and attention, the size of which left promoters around the globe sweating on their udgets. But Lewis brought the Santa Monica show with him and meetings ignored him at their peril. Variously labelled 'greedy', 'arrogant', certainly calculating", he has nevertheless, rarely failed to deliver. In his own country, which has virtually ignored the growing popularity of the sport, Lewis achieved a fame unheard of in track and field. In the rest of the world he became an icon.

Indeed, virtually the only achievement to have eluded him was the long jump world record but even then he did play his part in pushing his great rival and team-mate Mike Powell beyond Bob Beamon's magical mark at those fabulous World Championships in 1991. After all, a long jump competition without Carl Lewis was never really one worth winning.

Yet, for all his magnificence as an athlete, Lewis has never reached the hearts and souls of fans in the way he should have. Ed Moses accused him of lacking humility and that's possibly all it would have taken. He never really learned his lesson from the LA Games of 1984 when even his four golds couldn't stem the boos from the most partisan of American crowds.

Holding back the years

And, even when he lost, he won. In Seoul, in 1988, Lewis was forced to watch in horror from the silver medal position as the drug-riddled Ben Johnson took his sprint title. Lewis was convinced he had been the real winner and so it was proved. The pretenders to his throne came and went but still Lewis fought doggedly to hold back the years and defy the form books. In the end, he won that battle too.

Now it really is close to being over and, despite everything, the greatest champion of them all has managed to finish on his terms not on those of us who only sit and watch. He wants to get into broadcasting and enjoy his new house in Houston. As ever, he will pick and choose his events this season with the same care he's taken for the past 16 years. It will surely be a grand finale but you can be certain that Carl Lewis – the King of the quotes – will talk a great race right to the finishing line.

HIS FEET speak as eloquently as Michael Johnson's or Carl Lewis's, and he has a treasure trove of gold and a world record to prove it. But Donovan Bailey's

Olympic accomplishments in the 100m have been largely overlooked in the hype surrounding Johnson's double and Lewis's miraculous ninth gold medal.

In Canada, however, Bailey's victory in Atlanta meant they could finally start blotting out the stain of Ben Johnson's disgrace when he tested positive after winning the 1988 Olympic gold medal. In the post-Ben era, Canadian fans had turned away from athletics.

Bruny Surin finished fourth at the 1992 Games, yet he had almost no profile at home. 'I don't know that I would have survived the years that Bruny had to go through,' said Bailey, 'with people not knowing or caring about the fact that he was at the top of his sport.'

Huge endorsement deals

Bailey, too, struggled for recognition at home even after winning the World Championship in 1995. When he returned home to Canada from Gothenburg he and two British athletes who were visiting him, tried to get a local night club to waiver the $5 admission fee. 'I'm the world champion,' Bailey said.

'I don't care, it's still $5,' the doorman said.

The corporate sponsors are now flocking to Bailey's door. He has signed endorsement deals worth hundreds of thousands of dollars from Adidas, Coca-Cola, Air Canada, Kellogg's and Helene Curtis, and his asking price on the European Grand Prix circuit has shot up to $50,000 per appearance.

Now 29, Bailey came late to athletics. He lived with his mother in Jamaica until he was 12, then moved to Ontario, where his father settled after a divorce. Although he ran track in high school, his passion was basketball, which he also played while attending college. When

he graduated with a diploma in business, he established a small successful telemarketing firm in Oakville and went to work.

AS BAILEY EYES MORE GLORY . . .

Crazy

In 1991, he and some friends attended the national track championships in Montreal. 'It sounds crazy,' he says, 'but I was watching those guys and thought, 'I can run faster than that.' '

He decided to try, and was soon challenging Surin for national honours, but he was not setting the international scene afire. By 1994, he felt he needed a change, so he signed on with Dan Pfaff, a sprint specialist who coaches at the University of Texas in Austin. Pfaff regarded his new pupil as a world record waiting to happen – Bailey is all legs and shoulders, joined by an absurdly narrow 28-inch waist.

Bailey is propelled by the hard lessons of his father. Before he retired, George Bailey was a chemical worker at an Oakville plant that designed and manufactured wallpaper. 'My father was never satisfied with any job that I ever did,' Bailey says. 'I was taught to always push for something better. If I ever got 99 per cent in a test, there was still one more per cent I could get.'

Dumb jock

The elder Bailey did not immediately support his son's choice – he did not want him to be seen as a dumb jock. 'He wasn't too happy that I gave up my business,' Bailey says. 'He didn't see track as a career. But now he realises that I have a God-given talent that I won't have forever, and that I am doing a good job.'

Bright, articulate, and personable, Bailey is the antithesis of Johnson. He doesn't even seem to resent the taint his predecessor left on his sport. 'It's our job as athletes to change people's opinion,' he says. 'I can't change anything that Ben did.'

FROM RU:

OUT ON HER OWN ... Svetlana Masterkova was a class apart in 1996

Svetlana Masterkova was the revelation of last year and her victories in the 800 and 1500m in Atlanta were among the highlights of the Olympics. But she insists that that was just the beginning

DOUBLE Olympic champion Svetlana Masterkova has set herself tough new targets on the track this season.

The 28-year-old Russian won the Olympic 800 and 1500m titles this year before going on to set world records over the mile and 1000m. Now she seeks further gold and more records.

'I have not been a world champion yet and I would like to be,' Masterkova said. 'I want to improve my world records, set new ones and improve the times I did in the 800m this year.'

Targets have been an essential ingredient in Masterkova's success since she returned from a two-year injury lay-off. In 1993, mental stress and the constant injuries, which had required operations on both her Achilles tendons, left Masterkova fearing her body could take no more. 'I

simply had no strength left. I decided I had to have a break or I might never run again – a third Achilles operation would have been the end,' she said.

Masterkova did not resume training until 1995. But from then on she trained like a woman with a mission, determined to reduce quickly the weight she had gained during pregnancy and fearing injury could return to haunt her at any time.

'My husband told me to take it easy at first in training so that my muscles could take it,' she said. 'But then I trained as if I were training for the last time in my life. I knew this could be my last chance at the Olympics.'

Her success was all the more remarkable because she has had to juggle training with bringing up her daughter. Much of the time her husband, professional cyclist Asyat Saitov, was racing and training in Spain.

'I am very grateful to my mother. She helps all the time. She took a lot on her shoulders – helping with the cooking, the tidying up and looking after Nastya (Anastasia),' she said.

Masterkova won the bronze medal in last year's 800m European Indoor Championships and went to Atlanta confident of winning at least the bronze in the 800m final. She swept aside pre-race favourites Maria Mutola of Mozambique and Ana Fidelia Quirot of Cuba, moved into a clear lead with 70m to run, and won in 1:57.73.

THAT WINNING FEELING...
Masterkova wins the Olympic 800m

Easy

The 1500m final just five days later was easier, she said. Brimming with confidence, she sensed victory was hers after the semi-final. 'People were congratulating me even before the race and I was completely at ease. The 800m was a great stress but the 1500 just felt like doing the 800m again twice. It was the easiest race of my life,' she said.

She burst into the lead with 250m to go and won in 4:0.83, ahead of Gabriela Szabo of Romania and Austrian Theresia Kiesl.

Masterkova was less confident she could break world records but rose magnificently to the challenge. She knocked 3.05s off the world mile record in Zurich in August with a time of 4:12.56. Nine days later, she clocked 2:28.98 in Brussels to shave 0.36s off the 1000m mark.

'There is a photograph of me pointing at the clock after I set one of the records. People think I am showing off but I did it because I was so surprised I had broken it,' she said.

Wealth and Security

Success has brought wealth and security. Masterkova had only one sponsor before last summer but is now negotiating deals with two other firms. She was given $100,000 by Russian authorities for winning her gold medals, won a bonus of $50,000 plus a gold bar for her world record in Zurich and has picked up plenty more in appearance fees. Moscow authorities are giving her a new flat.

The secret of her success? 'Having no injuries and working hard,' she says.

There have been some slight drawbacks as well. 'Sometimes Asyat looks at me a bit differently and asks me if I am going to change. He probably thinks I will but I won't. I still clean up our apartment,' she said.

Masterkova rested after her year's toils and spent the winter months living and training near the Spanish town of Alicante with her husband.

One reason she needs to rest is to avoid strains or injuries which she still fears could force her out of action at any time. 'I still fear I may not have many seasons left. I don't think I could take any more operations,' she said.

Apart from her sporting aims, Masterkova dreams of having a second child but only after she hangs up her spikes. For now, she is looking forward to getting back to Spain, practising her Spanish and heading for a local restaurant where she enjoys singing karaoke.

OPEN MOUTH . . . Masterkova shows her joy at winning the 800m

NOTICEABLY *firmer* SKIN.

NIVEA body

SKIN FIRMING COMPLEX

BODY MOISTURISER
with
Natural Liposomes
& Vitamin E

NOTICEABLY FIRMER SKIN

NIVEA BODY SKIN FIRMING COMPLEX
contains a unique combination of active ingredients f
noticeably firmer skin. Natural liposomes carry safflow
oil to develop elasticity and tone. Vitamin E protects
your skin and helps to maintain moisture balance.

NIVEA BODY. FEEL GOOD ALL OVER.

the triathlon magazine
Everything you need to know about cross training

RUNNING
Training articles by **Julian Goater** Ex British 10,000m Champion (1982).

NUTRITION
Bar and Drink Reviews
Cutting Edge Science
Burning Fat, Carbo Loading
Healthy Eating, Supplements

MEDICAL
Problems Solved by Dr Rod Jaques, Medical Adviser to the BTA and member of the Olympic Medical Team.

PRODUCT REVIEWS
All the latest equipment tested, Running/Cycling Shoes, Bikes, Cycle Components, Swim Wear and much more

Send For A
Free
Back Issue Today
Just Complete The
Form Below Or Subscribe
Only £22 for 11 Issues

ABSOLUTE BEGINNERS
Starting From Scratch
Training & Racing Advice
Ask The Expert - Your Problems solved.

TEN YOUNG BRITS

IAN MACKIE

Event: 100m/200m
Age: 22
Club: Pitreavie AC

IAN MACKIE made giant leaps in 1996 when he progressed from being a promising 200m runner to an Olympic semi-finalist at 100m. Had a hamstring injury not forced him to scratch from that semi-final, he would surely have improved on his season's best of 10.17 sec. That time came when he carved his own special place in athletics history by becoming the first Briton to beat Linford Christie over 100m since 1986. A World Junior silver medallist in 1994, Mackie represented Scotland at 200m in the last Commonwealth Games. Now a part of Christie's Nuff Respect squad, Mackie can look forward to more improvement in 1997 after finishing his sensational Olympic season ranked No 3 in Europe.

ANGELA THORP

Event: 100m Hurdles
Age: 24
Club: Wigan Harriers

EMERGING from two years of injury and illness, Angie Thorp proved her undoubted pedigree with a series of personal bests and scintillating performances at the Olympic Games. Ranked tenth in the UK at the end of the 1995 season, the Yorkshire-born Thorp earned her spot on the Olympic team with victory at the AAA Championships. In Atlanta she excelled, clocking a new British record of 12.80 sec in finishing fifth in her semi-final. In 1995, her best time of 13.28 placed her sixteenth on the UK all-time list. By the end of last summer she was ranked sixteenth in the world.

IWAN THOMAS

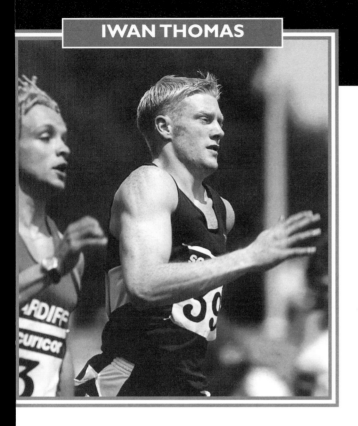

MARK HYLTON

Event: 400m
Age: 23
Club: Newham & Essex Beagles

Event: 400m
Age: 20
Club: Windsor, Slough & Eton

FOR a few glorious weeks in early 1996, Iwan Thomas found himself top of the world rankings, thanks to a 44.66 sec Welsh record run in the sunshine of South Africa. It was no fluke. He further established himself by confirming the Welsh record with 44.69 for third place in that epic AAA Championship race at the Olympic trials in Birmingham. And the previously unknown Thomas carried his form all the way to Atlanta to finish fifth in the 400m final won by the great Michael Johnson and help Britain's relay team win a silver medal.

AS IT used to be with British middle distance athletes, so it is now with 400m runners. Mark Hylton could find a place in any team in Europe except his own, such is the strength in depth over one lap. Nevertheless, he showed in 1996 – his first year as a senior – that he is still destined to make his mark. An outstanding teenager, he followed his fourth place at the 1994 World Juniors by winning his fourth English Schools title and by becoming the sixth Briton in succession to win the European Junior 400m gold in 1995. Sixth place in last summer's AAA final and Olympic trial earned him a trip to Atlanta as a member of the 400m relay squad.

DARREN CAMPBELL

Event: 100m/200m
Age: 23
Club: Sale Harriers

DARREN CAMPBELL is one of a group of British sprinters looking to fill the gap left by Linford Christie this summer. The most successful Briton ever at junior level, he was the first to win the sprint double at the European Juniors in 1991. He won silver medals at 100 and 200m in the following year's World Juniors. His progress in the senior ranks has been interrupted by injury and a two-year spell playing professional football with Plymouth, Newport FC and Weymouth. He returned to the athletics fold in 1996 and clocked a pb of 10.17 sec in Bratislava at the end of May only to narrowly miss out on an individual place in the Olympic team after a disastrous AAA's Championships.

JAMES BRIERLEY

Event: High Jump
Age: 19
Club: Telford AC

JAMES BRIERLEY was the top high jumper in the world for his age in 1996 but although he cleared 2.26m last summer, he could manage only seventh in the World Junior Championships in Sydney in August. Already highly experienced, with senior international appearances dating back to 1995, Brierley can expect to challenge established stars Steve Smith and Dalton Grant for domestic honours this summer. Twice a British Under-20 title holder, Brierley, a former English Schools champion, won a bronze medal at the 1995 European Juniors.

BEN CHALLENGER

Event: High Jump
Age: 19
Club: Charnwood AC

BEN CHALLENGER upset the form books last summer when he took the silver medal at the World Juniors in Sydney with a leap of 2.21m. Earlier Challenger, twice an English Schools champion, was second in the AAA Junior Championships. He goes into the 1997 season as a strong favourite for the European Junior title. A flamboyant character, he is sure to exite British crowds in the years ahead.

NATHAN MORGAN

Event: Long Jump
Age: 18
Club: Leicester Corinthian

THE massive improvement Nathan Morgan made in 1996 suggests that this year should see him installed as Britain's No 1 long jumper – an event crying out for a domestic success story. His best last summer was a wind assisted 7.97m, easily the best in Britain. Even so, his personal best of 7.74m, which won him the bronze medal at the World Juniors in Sydney, showed just how far he had come from 1995. An English Schools champion and AAA Junior title holder, he seems set to challenge the best in Europe.

DEAN MACEY

Event: Decathlon
Age: 19
Club: Old Gaytonians

BEING hailed as the best prospect since Daley Thompson could prove something of a handicap but Dean Macey has already shown that he's made of the right stuff. He improved by over 800 points in 1996 to earn a silver medal at the World Juniors in August. Coached by Greg Richards, a former British international and team-mate of Thompson's, Macey should have no problem handling his first year among the senior ranks. His strength lies in his all-round ability at the ten events although his bankers remain the high hurdles and the javelin.

JANINE WHITLOCK

Event: Pole Vault
Age: 23
Club: Trafford AC

A RELATIVE newcomer to the sport who became a British record holder in 1996. It was only a couple of years ago that Janine Whitlock began dabbling in sprinting but it was when she took up the pole vault that her athletics career took off. Ranked third in the UK with 3.60m in 1995, she assumed pole position in a season when she competed in some 50 competitions at home and abroad. In July she twice broke the British record, and became the first Briton to clear 4.00m at Telford in September. Extremely quick on the runway – she is no mean sprinter either – she is still learning and should continue the improvement this summer and take part in the first ever women's pole vault at the World Championships in Athens.

OFFICER OF THE WATCH
(IF SHE'D JOINED THE NAVY)

It's time to decide. Only a few years from now, you could be scrutinizing some office clock for that 5 o'clock reprieve. Or scrutinizing the horizon for approaching enemy warships. It's up to you. Join the Royal Navy and you could equally well become a Warfare Specialist, a Sea Harrier Pilot, a Communications Expert or any other of the dozens of jobs we offer.

The one thing they have in common is that they'll all stretch you to your limits. We'll train you to the highest standards to make sure you acquire highly-tuned skills. In a ship everyone is a key member of a team, so we can't afford to ignore your potential. If you have it in you, we'll bring it out.

Interested? Then find out more by sending off the coupon or calling us on 0345 300 123 now. If not, let's hope you find a seat on that bus home tonight.

READY TO TAKE YOU ON. AND ON. 0345 300 123

The Royal Navy is looking for men and women to fill vacancies now. Find out more at your local Jobcentre or send to: The Royal Navy and Royal Marines Careers Service, Dept BE81711, FREEPOST 4335, Bristol BS1 3YX. No stamp needed. http://www.royal-navy.mod.uk

Name (Mr, Mrs, Miss)_____

Address_____

Postcode_____ Date of birth_____

Telephone_____

Are you interested in being a Rating ☐ or an Officer ☐ (Please Tick)

We are equal opportunities employers under the Race Relations Act and welcome enquiries and applications from all ethnic groups. Normally you should have been a UK resident for the past five years.

PART THREE

YOUTH ATHLETICS

THE FACES OF

British athletics looks to be in safe hands with competitors of the talent of Tom Lerwil and Vicki Jamison to lead the sport into the next millennium. Here we profile Britain's Junior Athletes of 1996

Tom Lerwill

BRITAIN'S new World Junior silver medallist at 800m starts life as a senior athlete this summer. Tom Lerwill, voted the country's best junior athlete in 1996 by the British Athletics Writers' Association, has already been compared with the likes of Sebastian Coe and Steve Ovett but he wants none of it.

'I'd rather not be compared with these guys,' he said. 'It's happened to others in my position and none of them have come anywhere near achieving what those two did. Let people reserve judgement until I've done something worthwhile and, even then, put things into perspective. So much can happen in this sport and I'd rather not have the pressure of having to emulate Coe and Ovett.'

Son of Alan, the 1974 Commonwealth champion and Britain's last great long jumper, Lerwill – who turns 20 in May – is a major talent who wants to set his own pace this year. He knows the transition will be tough but his aim is to get into races where he can bring his personal best down from 1:47.27 to around 1:45 and finish in the first three.

'I want to improve gradually and not find myself totally outclassed in races where I finish seventh or eighth,' he said. 'That's no good to me.'

Guided by his dad, and coach, Glen Grant, Lerwill's main aim for the summer is a medal at the World Student Games, in Sicily, in August. Given Britain's paucity of talent over two laps, however, there is a chance that the youngster could make it to the

World Championships in Athens. 'That would be good,' he admitted. 'But I can't let that be a major target. It's a massive step up in class.'

Shifting targets

The Loughborough University student, who won gold with the 4x400m relay team at the 1995 European Junior Championships, began last season merely hoping to make the team for Sydney. When his summer – only his second as an 800m runner – kicked into action, so the target shifted.

'I was running well and when it became clear that I would make the team, I started to think about reaching the final. Then I felt so good through the heats that I lined up for the final seriously thinking about a medal. On reflection, it could so easily have been gold but I'm delighted with the silver.'

The only blip in a successful summer came when he was beaten in the AAA Junior Championships where Irishman James Nolan pipped him on the line.

Such has been his career on the track so far that he has never overreached his aspirations. As a schoolboy he represented Essex at cricket, hockey and rugby and did not start training seriously as an athlete until he was 17 years old.

'My dad has always been encouraging but he's never pushed me,' Lerwill said. 'Once I'd made the decision that I wanted to train seriously, it was all systems go. The last two years have gone well and dad's knowledge and

experience have been invaluable.'

He has already beaten some of Britain's best over 800m and he is set to take a few more scalps before the summer is over.

PEDIGREE COMPETITOR ... Tom Lerwill has benefited from his father's experience

THE FUTURE

SILVER LINING...
Jamison finished second in Sydney

Vicki Jamison

VICKI JAMISON is the first to admit she showed no real talent at athletics as an 11-year-old but, under the guidance of schoolteacher Alan Keys, she persevered. The result of her endeavours was a silver medal at last year's World Junior Championships and, at just 19 years old, national recognition as Northern Ireland's Woman Sports Personality of the Year.

The award was rightly presented by British Athletic Federation President Mary Peters, the 1972 Olympic pentathlon champion and the last woman from the Province to win a medal at a major championship. Now Jamison, 20 in May, enters the senior ranks this summer looking to follow in the footsteps of Sally Gunnell over 400m hurdles. Back in the days when Jamison was little more than an enthusiastic schoolgirl at her Friday afternoon athletics sessions, it was Gunnell, along with Kriss Akabusi, who provided the inspiration.

'They were the athletes I really admired,' she said. 'I wasn't very good at hurdling then but I enjoyed having a go and it was fun.'

She is still having fun, even during the winter when training with coach Brian Hall means gruelling sessions and speed endurance runs. 'It can be hard but I enjoy all the sessions,' Jamison said.

Fabulous summer

She enjoyed a fabulous summer in 1996, winning the national 400m title indoors before taking the Irish Universities 200m title and sharing the Inter-Counties 400m hurdles gold with Louise Fraser after a tie in the race in Bedford. She won more golds at the Northern Ireland Championships over 100 and 200m, both with personal bests and clocked her fastest ever time of 57.27 in winning the AAA Junior 400m hurdles title, a British junior record.

Before that, she achieved another ambition by racing against Sally Gunnell in the final of the AAA Championships and Olympic Trials in Birmingham, where she finished seventh. Her season ended with that glorious silver medal in Sydney. As well as recognition at home, she was duly named as the British Athletic Writers' Association female junior athlete of the year.

This year she has honed her speed with races indoors over 60m hurdles and 200m before embarking on a summer programme which should culminate at the Under-23 European Championships and World Student Games. There is an outside chance of selection for the World Championships in Athens but her realistic target on the bigger stage will be next year's Commonwealth Games.

This summer, too, she may return to sprint hurdling outdoors for the first time since she badly injured a foot going over the higher barriers in training two years ago. According to Hall, there is much more to come from Jamison.

'Last year she worked really hard and earned the rewards,' he said. 'Running against Sally for the first time in those Olympic Trials gave her a tremendous boost and we're looking forward to more races through 1997.'

CLEARING EVERY HURDLE...Vicki Jamison on her way to silver at the World Junior Championship.

GET INVOLVED -
THE REEBOK RACING CLUB MOVE
ON IN 1997

Do you ever feel there should be more to your athletics than just training on your own when you can fit it in? Would you like meet other athletes but can't match your local club's training time. Would you like help working towards your personal goals such as up-to-date information on developments in training methods or advice on diet, supplementary training aids or a specific problem?

If you answered Yes to any of the above, then read on - we can help.

The Reebok Racing Club was established in 1982 to help serious athletes like yourself, no matter what your performance level. At present, there are more than 4000 members - including runners, jumpers and throwers from all parts of Great Britain and Northern Ireland.

The club is a part of Reebok's long term commitment to the grass roots of the sport - including sponsorship of Sports Hall Athletics, the Inter-Counties Cross Country Champs and the Area and National Six and Twelve Stage Relays.

As a club member you receive a FREE high quality Reebok Racing Club T-shirt (in itself worth the joining fee) and a full colour quarterly newsletter - The Racing Club Magazine - which contains articles on training and new technologies in the sport, interviews with well-known and not-so-well-known athletes, informed opinion, competitions and special reader offers. Other club benefits include training advice from top coaches such as Bruce Tulloh, and discounts on kit at specialist retailers.

In 1997 the club will enhance its membership benefits. Newly appointed manager Tim Hutchings, an Olympian, World Cross Country and Commonwealth Games medallist, is planning affordable training days and weekends away in locations such as Wales, the Lake District and the New Forrest. He is also developing a warm-weather training package to cater for the tastes, needs and budgets of as many members as possible.

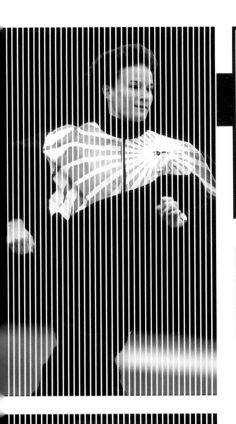

The National Schools Championships

MARK HYLTON is one of the world's top 400m runners and a member of the British relay squad that won silver in Atlanta last year. But he had already competed in the Olympics – the 'Schools Olympics'

I competed in the English Schools Championships and the Atlanta Olympic Games in consecutive years so the memories are still very clear in my mind.

In 1995, approaching my last English Schools, I was the clear favourite to retain my senior boys 400m title and with a personal best of 46.37 the record of 46.30 was well within my grasp. Having won the AAA under-20 200m in a personal best of 21.09 – in the first round – and due to compete in the AAA Championships a week later, I was on a high and raring to go

When I arrived in Nottingham I was focused on leaving with the record under my belt. Not even being randomly drawn in lane one for the final was going to faze me. In the end I went out hard and maintained form down the home straight, crossing the line in 46.26, happy to have retained my title on the way.

That experience helped me prepare for the bigger task ahead as I set about earning my place in Britain's team for Atlanta, which I managed to achieve and pick up a silver medal as a member of the 4x400m squad.

Excellent organisation

The English Schools is often described as the 'Schools Olympics' due to the excellent organisation, timekeeping and sheer scale of it. You get billeted a the home of local families and helpers. I was lucky to get friendly people each time and this helped me with my preparations.

My first English Schools competition was back in 1991. On that occasion I was racing over 200m in Stoke. Luckily for me, the two quickest boys at the distance – Kevin and Cephus Howard – ran in different events because you car only compete in individual race and one relay. I raced to victory in a personal best of 23.40, winning the gold medal by one-hundredth of a second. After that, I really felt that my career was on its way.

> **I raced to victory in a personal best of 23.40, winning the gold medal by one-hundredth of a second. After that, I really felt that my career was on its way.**

At Hull the following year I wised up to the fact that 200m was not my prime event. I had run a couple of good 400m but was entered at the shorter sprint for the inter-boys event. A half-second improvement to 22.91

ANFARE FOR THE SPECIAL ATHLETE: The English Schools is a special occasion in any athletic career

vas not good enough to get me ny further than the semi-finals nd I crossed the line convinced f the need to concentrate on the quarter-mile.

That decision paid off because n Blackpool in 1993 I comfortably von the inter-boys 400m in 49.10, hough my main memory is of now a strong sea breeze hindered ast times. There had been a lot of elevision and magazine coverage round Guy Bullock and his sucessful assault on David Grindley's enior boys 400m record. Later on hat summer, Guy became the latest in a long line of British juniors o win the European Junior 400m itle.

Point to prove

Having raced senior internationals, ncluding Curtis Robb and Nigel Will at British League level, I still

> **The British support for athletics in Atlanta was great. Every time a British athlete was competing, I was overwhelmed by the amount of Union Jacks flying.**

TASTE OF THINGS TO COME:
The English Schools can often lead to greater things

continue my squad's record of being represented at every European Junior Championships since 1987.

By the time of the 1994 English Schools Championships in Telford I was back on the winning trial. Bullock and Nick Budden were considered my major threats but I was confident of my own ability. The weekend before the Schools I had won the AAA Junior Championships in a best ever 46.94 – with Budden on my tail.

At Telford I felt I had nothing left to prove but was keen to maintain my unbeaten record against junior opposition. I took the race to the rest and won in 47.09.

Annoying

I suppose that one of the main differences between the English Schools and the Olympic Games is that in the former you cannot secure a better lane draw by performing well in the qualifying

"Although nothing can prepare you fully for the pressure of the Olympic Games the Schools help you face up to the pressure"

had to prove my candidature for the European Junior Championships and was hopeful of securing a 4x400m spot. As a youth, I had passed on the AAA Junior Championships because it fell just two days after I had returned from the World School Games with two gold medals and a new 400m personal best of 48.48 and was tired from the travelling. My coach said break 48 seconds. My only chance of securing a place came at the Schools Home International in Dublin. I ran 47.81, a championship best performance, but it was not good enough and I was very disappointed not to rounds. It can be a bit annoying to be the best on paper and the quickest in the qualifying, only to be drawn in lane one or eight in the final. That happened to me in both Telford and Nottingham, but it only made me more determined to win and secure the championship record.

Best Kids' type chants and had come fully prepared to stand up for our county!

In addition, the accommodation was very similar. While the Olympics provide a number of facilities to help you to use up spare time – shops, arcades, cinemas, concerts and restaurant chains – the sleeping quarters were nothing special. At Blackpool, Telford and Nottingham, the Berkshire team were billeted at university sites and these were of similar or better quality than available in Atlanta.

Although nothing can prepare you fully for the pressure of the Olympic Games, the team management and spirit created at Schools athletics helps you to face up to the challenges and enabled me to come to terms with Atlanta.

The British support for athletics in Atlanta was great. Every time a British athlete was competing, I was overwhelmed by the amount of Union Jacks flying. I know this spurred all of us on and is something we can be

But the two events are very similar in many aspects. Firstly, they both adopt a regimented approach to timetabling events and require that athletes have the self-discipline to prepare themselves and arrive ready to compete at the allotted time. Secondly, at their respective levels, they both have a large vocal element and patriotism, which serves to lift everyone to better performances. Tribal songs added to the atmosphere of the English Schools, and the Berkshire posse had their own anthem that was used to create a strong team spirit before the Championships. We expected the usual 'West Mids, proud of. Past venues for the English Schools Championships may not compare to the likes of Barcelona, Atlanta and Sydney, but the English Schools *is* the Schools Olympics.

MARK HYLTON

By Tom Knight

When the young Mark Hylton broke Roger Black's ten year-old British junior record in winning the 1995 AAA Indoor title, he was excited enough. When he received a congratulatory phone call from the man himself, the pleasure he felt at his achievement was complete.

It was typical of Black to encourage a talented junior and it has been equally typical of Hylton that he improved quickly enough to claim a silver medal as part of Britain's successful 400m relay squad at last year's Olympic Games.

Now Black, a silver medallist in the individual event in Atlanta and rightfully acclaimed as national No1 after more than a decade at the top, is doing his bit to ensure Hylton's future progress. Two years after that initial phone call, Hylton now trains alongside Black, hurdler Jon Ridgeon and Windsor team-mate Mark Richardson in a group intent on capitalising on last season's success.

His coach, Martin Watkins, is in no doubt about the effect the association with Black has had. 'Back in the winter of 1995 Mark had lowered Roger's record to 46.56 sec and was already feeling pretty pleased with himself. Roger's call was confirmation that he had achieved something special and he felt very proud of himself. It was, though, only the start for Mark and he's been careful to keep his feet on the ground and work hard for the improvement he's shown.'

Hylton is no ordinary talent. He dominated youth and junior one-lap running since he turned to it after giving up the pentathlon – he was Southern champion at 15. He even gave up playing football for Slough Town's youth team to dedicate himself to athletics. He was World Schools champion in 1993, the same year that he became English Schools Intermediate and National Youth champion. The following year he was English Schools Senior champion and was disappointed to finish only fourth at the World Juniors – although he won a bronze medal in the relay.

But, after his success on the boards in 1995, he enjoyed the best of summers and remained unbeaten by any junior in the world over 200m, 300m and 400m. Denied the chance to double up at the European Juniors in Hungary, Hylton clocked 45.97 to became the sixth successive Briton to lift the 400m title, following in the illustrious footsteps of Black – of course – Peter Crampton, Wayne McDonald, David Grindley and Guy Bullock. He won his second gold medal of the Championships in the relay.

He was part of the European Cup gold medal winning relay team and secured selection for the Gothenburg World Championships by finishing second behind Richardson at the trials. At just 18, he travelled to Sweden as the youngest team member by a good three years.

Further success followed in 1996. The indoor season saw him win the AAA 400m title but his aim was to claim a place in the team bound for the Centennial Olympic Games. Sixth place in an epic AAA final at the official trials in Birmingham, in which Black again broke the British record, was enough.

And so a new era opened up for the prodigious talent who couldn't afford to buy his first pair of running spikes without help from his local council lottery. A winter's training alongside Black, Ridgeon and Richardson opened his eyes to new possibilities. 'The benefits of training with the group will come out in years to come,' said Watkins. 'They're a great bunch of guys and just being with them will help make Mark a more rounded person as well as a better athlete. Roger's had his injuries and health scares over the years and Jon's comeback after his problems are a constant source of inspiration for any youngster with his sights set on the very top.'

As for Hylton, he feels the benefit of the training sessions every time he takes part. 'I used to train too often in the comfort zone,' he said. 'Now I come away from sessions feeling terrible but I know the hard work will pay off. The 400 metres is Britain's strongest event in depth in this country but we know that to get the best out of ourselves and even beat the Americans at major championships, we have to help each other.'

Hylton goes into the summer after a two-month training stint in sunny California and with two goals in mind. The first is to challenge for a place in the World Championship relay team; the second to run inside 45 seconds. Both are attainable.

With a GNVQ in tourism and leisure from the East Berkshire College under his belt, he's taken a year out to capitalise on his exceptional talent. He might even take more than a year. After all, there's a European Championships and Commonwealth Games year on the horizon and much more to come from Mark Hylton.

EPILEPSY

At the mention of the word some people run a mile.

On the other hand, some people go to even greater lengths to help.

Rosemary Natrajan has epilepsy and she plans to cycle over 5,000 miles across **Canada** to help people with epilepsy.

Rosemary is a 52 year old retired nurse who had to take up cycling as a means of carrying the shopping home. Vancouver to Halifax, Nova Scotia, seem a long way to go to get a tin of beans!

Rosemary plans to leave Vancouver on her Dawes Super Galaxy bicycle in early May 1997.

Each year dozens of people run over 26 miles in the London, and other Marathons, to help people with epilepsy.

If you already have a place in the London Marathon you might like to receive our sponsorship pack.

Whether you run, jump or throw, you may think that your sporting prowess could be used to help those less fortunate than you. If so, contact us to discuss your ideas.

If, like Rosemary, you or your club would like to help others less fortunate than yourselves, contact:

The National Society for Epilepsy, Chalfont St Peter, Gerrards Cross, Bucks, SL9 0RJ
Tel: 01494 601414

The National Society for Epilepsy

Looking forward to conquering epilepsy

Epilepsy is one of the oldest conditions known to man having been identified over 4,000 years ago. It is the most common serious neurological condition affecting up to 500,000 people in the UK.

Anyone can get it at any time of their lives - Rosemary Natrajan got it when she was 46 years old. It affects 1 in 20 families and there is no cure except delicate and sensitive brain surgery in a very few cases.

A diagnosis of epilepsy can have a devatating effect on the individual and their family. It can lead to losing a driving licence which might mean losing a job. Added to this is the stigma and prejudice surrounding epilepsy, born of centuries of myth, fear and ignorance. It's not surprising that many people hide the fact that they have epilepsy.

The National Society for Epilepsy has a 105 year track record fighting this misunderstood and often frightening condition. We are a world class centre of excellence recognised by the World Health Organisation (WHO), one of only six such centres in the world.

The Society provides the most comprehensive range of services for people with epilepsy anywhere. These services include the largest and most active epilepsy research programme, the only brain scanner dedicated to epilepsy in the world, the biggest epilepsy clinic in Europe, longer term and respite care, rehabilitation, community based supported housing, a dedicated telephone helpline, professional and lay people training courses, community based specialist nurse training, videos, books, leaflets, multi-media computer aided learning and self-help community groups.

We need help if we are to maintain our standards status as a world class centre of excellence.

The British Athletes Association formally launched itself on December 16, 1996. At a press conference in London, a group of Britain's leading competitors committed themselves to accepting a much greater role in the decision-making and delivery of our sport.

The focus of everyone's thoughts, however, could be summed up in the opening press statement and key objective of the organisation, namely:

"We wish to represent the views of BRITISH athletes, hence the title of the Association; thus we fully support the BRITISH Athletic Federation and their professional staff in their role as the governing body of BRITISH athletics."
BAA BOARD MEMBERS

"The sport, the sponsors, the spectators, the officials and most importantly, the athletes can only benefit from the new partnership between the BAA and BAF."
Steve Backley

"The sport has had a rough time in the last few years but now I feel really excited about the future. Perhaps more importantly I feel involved for the first time."
Denise Lewis

"As a director of the BAA, I now understand far more about how our sport works. By the same token I am now far more aware of how big a responsibility we have taken on and I'm conscious of having to represent all athletes, not just myself."
Jonathan Edwards

"The formation of new partnerships in athletics will push forward the rapidly changing boundaries and expectations of all those involved in our sport. By integrating disabled athletes within the current structure, athletics will not only be at the forefront of progressive governing bodies in the UK, but will pull together the vast amount of knowledge and help all athletes achieve their best."
Tanni Grey

"This is the greatest ever opportunity for all athletes to become involved at the centre of the decision-making process of our sport rather than being kept on the outside, largely uninformed."
Roger Black

BRITISH ATH
COME AND JOIN U

AT the heart of the Association is the Board of Directors, made up of some of Britain's top athletes.

During the last 18 months, they have all given up a great deal of their time in order to bring about the BAA and to initiate the much-needed change within the sport.

It should also be said that this time has been given freely. Only Geoff Parsons, as the Board's full time employee, is remunerated for his time.

Much of this change will be brought about due to the new, jointly shared company between the athletes and the Federation, in charge of the televised events and their related commercial activities (once again with both the BAF and BAA directors giving their time freely). Confidence in the new company is growing daily as the commercial partners of the sport begin to realise the opportunities opening up, with the new atmosphere being created between athletes and administrators.

The flexibility and ability of this new company to make mutually agreed decisions has already borne fruit for the whole of British Athletics with the new exclusive television contract with Channel 4.

The members of the BAF Council deserve considerable praise for voting to deliver much of the new structure. It was noticeable that not one person opposed the motion.

At long last, a unified sport is beginning to emerge with the obvious partnership between administrators, athletes,

> "The importance of athletes everywhere and the British Athletes Association cannot be underestimated.
>
> "Certainly the fact that the athletes, through the BAA, were going to be partners in the project made us even more interested in getting involved.
>
> "We believe in long-term relationships in which we work together with a sport. But if all we could was reproduce the same old boring BBC/ITV coverage, or if we were uncertain about the commitment of the top stars to British athletics then there would have been no point.
>
> "I would say the fact that the BAA was so enthusiastic about helping to find new ways to bring athletics up to date, to let viewers behind the scenes to give them an understanding of what really goes on, and to become intimately involved with both the events and the TV production process, helped clinch the deal."
>
> Mike Miller - Commissioning Editor, Sports and Special Events, Channel 4

sponsors and television strengthening daily.

The Athletes Association is still learning and growing as an organisation. Although only a small number of services will be initially provided by the BAA, this will undoubtedly grow over the coming year, making the attraction of membership even greater for everyone.

Without doubt the most important features will be the newsletter (which will contain information to help athletes about the sport and the people in it) and the personal membership card containing the Association's telephone number, allowing athletes direct access to the centre of the decision-making process of the sport.

With the likelihood of significant National Lottery funding coming through the sport, it is also essential that athletes are helped to understand the implications and responsibilities involved and have their own organisation, lobbying and working on their behalf.

The British Athletes Association is there for every athlete in this country to gain benefit from. It is a place for athletes to talk with each other in an environment of trust and openness. It is an organisation that will listen to you and be influenced by you.

We welcome your applications for membership and hope we are able to listen and serve in order to bring about the brightest possible future for athletes and athletics in this country.

Geoff Parson

TES ASSOCIATION
WE ARE AT YOUR SERVICE

WHAT YOU GET
Initially all new members will receive:

- Free BAA T-shirt • Membership card
- Newsletter containing *competitions, information, features, special offers.*
- Free help and advice line.

Many further services are being considered for delivery through the Association, from sponsors, TV and BAF. These will be announced as available but range from insurance, financial and legal services through to media training and athletic education courses.

MEMBERSHIP APPLICATION FORM

Surname	Forename
Date of Birth	Sex
Home Address	Occupation
	Term Address (if applicable)
Home Telephone	Work Telephone
Mobile Number	Fax Number
E-Mail	

Are you:	an athlete	an official	a coach	a supporter

Event(s)	Personal best(s)
Event(s)	Personal best(s)
Event(s)	Personal best(s)
Club(s): 1st claim	Club(s): 2nd claim

Please tick the category of Membership for which you are applying (for guidance see attached article)

Athlete Services Trust (£20 per annum)	International (£12 per annum)
Member (£8 per annum)	Associate (£15 per annum)

Please make cheques payable to the British Athletes Association

Please tick the size of T-shirt you require   XL   L   M   S

I confirm that, to the best of my knowledge, all of the above information is correct

Signature   Date

Please return this form to this address: The British Athletes Association Limited, 2 Alexandra Mews, Tamworth, Staffordshire B79 7HT

THE BRITISH ATHLETES ASSOCIATION
MEMBERSHIP CATEGORIES

Athlete Service Trust
This category of membership will be related to future announcements with regard to these athletes named in the final UK Sports Council approved version of the British Athletic Federation National Performance Development Plan. Athletes in this category will have their membership upgraded automatically, in the first year, at no extra cost.

International
Any athlete who is currently a fully paid up member of an affiliated athletic club (either junior or senior) who has had an indoor or outdoor representative Great Britain & Northern Ireland international since January 1, 1992. Eligibility is to be authenticated in conjunction with the British Athletic Federation on a four-year rolling basis, reviewed at the end of each year.

Member
Any athlete, from any age group, who is a current fully paid up member of an affiliated athletic club in the UK and a British citizen.

Associate
Any person with an interest in athletics, either from the UK or abroad, who is not a current competing athlete. This category is open to coaches, officials and supporters (overseas members may be subjected to a £10 annual surcharge to cover the additional cost of postage).

The Board of Directors of the British Athletes Association reserve the right of final acceptance of any membership application.

THE FUTURE IS BRIGHT . .

WITH so many other sports such as football, gymnastics, rugby and swimming attracting Britain's youngsters these days it is encouraging to see the number of new age group athletics records set during 1996.

No fewer than 11 sets of new figures are nestled at the top of the listings which go right through the age groups, although it is noticeably stronger in the under-17 boys' and girls' categories which augers well for the next couple of years, at least. So one can perhaps say that British Athletics is set for a bright future.

But what if these new record holders are attracted to the more lucrative sports around? This has been the case with some of the brighter sprinters for instance, having been lured away to much-promised mega bucks of rugby union. And there are so many other youngsters already toying with football – the nation's national sport – hoping it will pay rich dividends.

Choices

At the TSB English Schools' AA Schools' Cup Final – a competition in which the school gains the honours rather than the individual – three of the individual winners already play at least three other sports. And two, at the tender age of 14, found themselves in the not so enviable position of having two schools matches on the same day, thereby having to make a choice.

So what is the governing body of British athletics doing in an attempt to keep the sport alive and running into the next millennium and beyond?

For one, they have tried and been successful in initiating a scheme for the under-13 age group which they hope will allow for some kind of fun element as well as a non-specialist and broad-based competition.

Fun in athletics is not new to the sport with various schemes already well and truly engraved in the annual programme, not least Sports Hall Athletics, which in 1995 saw a massive increase in primary school participation for the under-11 age group with approximately 60,000 children, and this year it has proved just as successful.

As it is the time for change is it time for the sports governing body to consider taking a leaf out of the books of football, tennis and gymnastics and other European countries by introducing a centre of excellence, where youngsters are given the opportunity to study at length their chosen sport. Up and down the country there are specialist schools where children as young as eight are put through their paces and taught the rules of the game. These centres have great financial backing from the Government. That's the difference because up until now athletics doesn't.

LATE BLOOMER . . . Sally Gunnell did not specialise as a youngster

Gunnell a great example

The way I see the new initiative set up by BAF's Track and Field Commission, which is due to begin in 1998, is an attempt to allow the youngsters to try every event and not to specialise too early.

It's not a bad thing to try everything going. Look at Sally Gunnell

he began her career as a multi-
venter and long jumper and it
asn't until she was about 18 that
e decided it was time to specialise
d chose the sprint hurdles. At the
ge of 22 she progressed from the
00m hurdles to the 400m hurdles,
d before her much publicised
eel injury she was even contem-
lating swapping events further to
e 800m.

So as you can see, the BAF have
nly the youngsters and their
ture – and ultimately the future
f the sport – at heart by enforcing
ew rules including:

Competition should be informal,
low-key and local with a flexible
format

Sub-regional competition could
be provided occasionally with
maximum travelling of three
hours

Leagues on a local level but with
no promotion and relegation

The main geographic basis for
competition should be the county. Trips to venues should be no
longer than 90 minutes

The age group should stand
alone – under-13s will not be
able to compete in under-15
competition

Annual area championships could
be introduced but there will be no
provision at national level

A mixed programme of some
single event competitions and
regular run, jump and throw
opportunities will be introduced
to emphasise developing a basic
competence in aspects of running, throwing and jumping.

SHOP WINDOW ... British athletics needs a successful youth scheme to ensure its future

It all sounds reasonable for the
sport to be looking after its future
but possibly the present junior
league system could suffer.

Take the McDonald's Young
Athletes' League, a well-established
system and one that is eagerly
fought out year after year by clubs
who believe it's a great honour to
be champions. It's a league which
is contested throughout the British
Isles from the under-17, under-15
to the under-13 age groups, boys
and girls. When this new non-specialist and broad-based structure
becomes reality the YAL, as it's
affectionately known, will presum-
ably have to take on a new format.

Will they have to exclude competition for the under-13 age
group, leaving a two-age-group
format, or will they have to totally
restructure altogether? Whichever
is the case will the new format be
quite so attractive to present and
prospective sponsors? One can
only wait and see. If it isn't, the
loser will be athletics.

Silver lining

As with the seniors in Atlanta, 1996
has not been a golden year, but
there's definitely been a silver
lining. The Great Britain juniors
travelled to the Southern
Hemisphere to *Sydney* for their
major event of the season, the
World Junior Championships and
four of the five individual
medallists exceeded all expectations
and came home with a clutch of silver and bronze medals.

Even though no junior man has
set a UK record since Steve Smith
broke the world record with a
2.37m high jump in 1992, there is
no doubt there's some outstanding
talent coming through.

Men's long jumping in Britain
hasn't really had anything to talk
about since Lynn Davies' British
record in June 1968 but Nathan
Morgan who, despite an injured
ankle, sailed out to a windy 7.97m
in the TSB English Schools' at
Sheffield, looks ready to challenge

Davies' record in the future. This performance, and winning the AAA U20 Championships, set him up for bronze in Australia and No1 spot in the 1996 UK senior rankings. A marvellous achievement, and he's still a junior for the 1997 season.

Two-lap running in this country has long been lingering in the doldrums since the heady days of Coe, Ovett, Cram and Elliott but with the emergence of Tom Lerwill Britain can begin to look forward with relish. Lerwill reduced his personal best down to 1:47.27 in his semi-final, and, after a lengthy phone call to his coach in Britain, he started his final full of confidence and with a specific plan. He came home with a much-deserved silver.

Daley Thompson set the ball rolling in multi-event terms in the 1970s, and now Dean Macey continues the line and improving his personal best by a whopping 818 points to win World Junior silver, the finest achievement by a British multi-eventer since Thompson's gold in 1977.

Fine performance

On the women's front Vicki Jamison emerged as the pretender to Gunnell's crown with her British junior 400m hurdles record of 57.27 in winning the World Junior silver. This performance alone is regarded as the finest by a Briton since the discipline's introduction in the late 1970s.

Pole vaulter Rhian Clarke set ten UK records but had no chance to compete in Australia because the event was not on the programme, while long jumper *Sarah Claxton* improved her personal best from 6.01m to 6.34m and was unbeaten by any Briton throughout the year.

Among the 38-strong team there were five under-17s and whatever success the under-20 age group gained the under-17s matched and some say bettered. The age group brimmed with class which was the most outstanding for many years. Here's looking to the future.

LEAP INTO THE FUTURE . . . Sarah Claxton is one of our most promising youngsters

BRITISH AGE GROUP RECORDS SET DURING 1996

RECORD BREAKERS . . . Carl Myerscough (top) and David Baker (right)

U17 men	400m Hurdles:	Richard McDonald 52.81
	Shot:	*Carl Myerscough* 18.40(i) / 21.20
	Javelin:	*David Parker* 68.26 (senior implement)/ 73.56 (U17 implement)
U20 women	400m Hurdles:	Vicki Jamison 57.27
	Pole Vault:	Rhian Clarke 3.65(i) / 3.70
	5km Walk:	Sarah Bennett 14:39.24(i)
U15 girls	Pole Vault:	Fiona Harrison 3.20(i)/3.50
U13 girls	Javelin:	Samantha Redd 36.06

PART FOUR

OFF THE TRACK

BROWN VICTORY CAPS GOOD YEAR FOR CROSS COUNTRY

British cross country running made big strides last year with Jon Brown's gold medal winning performance in the European Championships – the icing on the cake

GOLDEN BROWN ... Jon Brown (no 58) on his way to victory at the European Championships

JON BROWN capped a year in which he established himself as Britain's best cross country runner by winning the third European Championships at Charleroi in Belgium in December.

The 25-year-old Bridgend-born resident of Vancouver, skipped across the clinging mud on what was a gloriously traditional course to become the first British man to win a major cross country gold medal since Ian Stewart took the world title in 1975. It was a remarkable achievement, made even more spectacular by the margin of victory. Brown, who finished twelfth and first European in March's World Cross Country Championships in South Africa, finished 35 seconds clear of Paulo Guerra of Portugal, winner of the title in 1994 and 1995.

Brown's performance should have led the way to a first ever British victory in the team race, with Keith Cullen, Andrew Pearson and Spencer Barden – who earned his selection after winning the Safeway International at Gateshead in November to end a six-year winning run by Kenyans – all in the top 30 after the first lap of the hilly

circuit. But first Cullen pulled out on the second lap, suffering the after-effects of a bout of flu and then Pearson fell back to leave the way open for the Portuguese to retain the title they won in 1995. Britain's men eventually finished just outside the medals.

Back in the hunt

No such disappointment for the women's scoring trio of Hayley Haining, Andrea Whitcombe and Suzanne Rigg. They finished with the bronze medals behind France

and Romania, with the 24-year-old Haining, back in the hunt after battling persistent injury problems since 1992, top scorer in ninth place.

The juniors too had a good day in their non-championship races. Sam Haughian and Amber Gascoigne, both only 17, finished sixth and fourth respectively.

The women's team was, of course, missing top names, Paula Radcliffe and Alison Wyeth. Both performed exceptionally throughout the year, only to miss out in he race that really mattered at the World Championships.

Radcliffe won the last race of 1995, eld her fitness over Christmas and uly beat Kenya's Rose Cheruiyot to ake the Coca Cola International at Mallusk in January. But, just when looked as if the 1992 World unior champion was set to make a

Suzanne Rigg won the Reebok Inter-Counties Championships in Luton, while Steffan White (Coventry Godiva), Amanda Wright (Shaftesbury Barnet), Tim Dickinson (Blackheath Harriers), Lucy Elliott (Shaftesbury Barnet), Martin Jones (Horwich) and Angie Hulley (Leeds) all became area champions.

Pearson, Chris Sweeney, Adrian Passey and John Nuttall. Wyeth took advantage of Radcliffe's absence to take her first major cross country title.

Later in the month, the English National, for so long the most important race of the year for enthusiasts, saw Nuttall put his World Championship aspirations on the line. Ignoring the advice of British team manager, Dave Clarke, to give the race a miss, he romped home the winner by 20 seconds

COMEBACK KID . . . Hayley Haining

BEST OF BRITISH . . . Keith Cullen

TOP OF THE WORLD . . . Paul Tergat won his second World Cross Country title

ahead of John Sherban over the gruelling nine-mile course at Newark. Pearson dropped out with a stitch. Spencer Duval, the defending champion, had to miss the race altogether because of injury. Bingley Harriers took the team title for the third time in six years. The club, famous as mud and glory specialists, won the English National Relay Championships a week later at Mansfield where the victorious women's team from Sale included Diane Modhal, in her first major race since winning her appeal against her drugs ban.

For the second year running, an American finished first in the women's National but New Yorker Nnenna Lynch's five-second victory over Wyeth was subsequently ruled out when it was discovered her club, Oxford University, had not registered her as an overseas athlete. Lynch was disqualified and so it was that Wyeth's unenviable run of five successive runners-up medals was ended by default.

In a year which saw mixed fortunes for British runners, Dave Clarke nominated Brown and

erious assault on the senior title, njury struck again. A troublesome back restricted Radcliffe's preparations and she could finish only nineteenth, albeit as leading Briton, in the race in Cape Town won by Gete Wami of Ethiopia. Brown's performance in the men's event that day was the best by a Briton since Tim Hutchings' silver medal seven years previously. Britain's men finished fifth, the women eleventh.

Earlier in the winter, Irishman ohn Downes and Warrington's

Bobby Quinn (Kilbarchan) and Debbie Kilner (Aberdeen) won their first ever Scottish titles at Irvine, Christian Stephenson and Wendy Ore (both Cardiff) won the Welsh and Dermot Donnelly (Annadale Striders) and Jill Bruce (Dromore) won the Northern Ireland titles.

First major title for Wyeth
Keith Cullen, who was to succumb to heat exhaustion in the World Championships, won the BAF Championship and trial for World Championships in March, ahead of

MUD QUEEN...Alison Wyeth (no 49) won the British Cross Country title from Liz Talbot (no 46) and Angie Hulley (no 18)

Radcliffe as his athletes of the year and sounded a warning for athletes and officials who might be looking for further success.

Back into the fold

'Jon ran a superb race in Belgium,' he said. 'Here was an athlete who, 12 months before, felt that there had been a change in cross country running in Britain and that he wanted to be a part of it. He came back into the fold and the benefits he enjoyed were obvious when he ran so well in Atlanta. He certainly did his bit to put British distance running back on track.

'Don't forget that half of the team from the World Cross Country Championships qualified for the Olympics in a year when British endurance running returned to its roots. Cross country is still a major part of an endurance athlete's base training and the lads who performed so well through the winter took their form into the summer.

'Paula is the best female distance runner in Britain. Injury hampered her in Cape Town but in the summer she went on to run well in the Olympic final and break Zola Budd's British 5000m record.

'There was so much flack over the team selection for Charleroi but we picked the most talented people available. The great thing is that they are all quite young. I was disappointed for Keith Cullen because he has been so unlucky in big races. It was the heat in Cape Town, the flu in the Europeans. Andrew Pearson was caught out because he was preparing specifically for the Worlds and was less race fit than he usually is at that time of the year.

'We saw yet again that it is easier to be successful at the Olympics than the World Cross Country Championships. But if we are to continue the improvement in this country then athletes must start to look at domestic titles again. Part of the process of learning to race at international level must include running in races like the Inter-Counties and the National where you can prove you are the best in your own country. The top runners can learn so much about pressure and having to fight for your own self-respect when the onus really is on you to get among the medals.

'If this area of the sport is to thrive then it needs funding and the best way to secure that is through success, at home and abroad.'

RADCLIFFE READY TO MOVE UP A STEP

Paula Radcliffe was once again Britain's outstanding female distance runner in 1996 but she is growing frustrated at missing out on the medals

AN OUTSTANDING junior and now one of Britain's most exciting talents, Paula Radcliffe managed to achieve excellence on two fronts in 1996. Her summer began with a first class honours degree in European Studies from Loughborough University and ended with a win in the Fifth Avenue Mile in New York City.

In between came a succession of fine performances on the track culminating in a magical week in August during which she shattered the British 5000m record held by Zola Budd.

But her athletic prospects had looked so different back in April when injury threatened her all-important Olympic build-up. A six-week break from running meant that she started the summer season late, having missed vital basic speed work. Nevertheless, with the qualifying time already under her belt after a fabulous 1995, she duly won the AAA Championship trial in fine style.

Her first Olympic Games provided her with a mixture of emotions. The climate and poor organisation in Atlanta brought their own problems. Prone to exercise-induced asthma, she was already taking three times her normal dose of medication and a combination of her own nerves and high humidity caused her to drink too much water before her first race.

Changing pace

The final was hard because the pace was constantly changing,' she said. In the end, the time in that race

ONE OF THE BEST . . . Paula Radcliffe (no 1) was once again Britain's top distance runner

wasn't relevant. I ran my worst time of the year but it was far from my worst race. At one stage I thought I might have managed the bronze medal but I missed the break.'

As China's Wang Junxia won the first ever Olympic 5000m title, 23-year-old Radcliffe finished fifth – just as she had done in the World Championships a year earlier.

And then came that week of personal bests. In Monte Carlo she clocked 8:37.07 for 3000m – the fifth fastest ever by a Briton – and in Zurich she played her part in Svetlana Masterkova's world record in the mile, finishing in 4:24.94. Two days later she lowered Budd's 11-year-old British 5000m record to 14:46.76 in Cologne.

'Everything seemed to come together that week and I suppose it

proved to me that I wasn't quite at my best in Atlanta,' Radcliffe said.

It also confirmed her status among the world's élite distance runners. Used to winning titles as a junior – most notably the World Cross Country Championship in Boston in 1992 – she aims to get among the medals at the World Championships in Athens. 'I'm tired of finishing fourth or fifth in the really big races,' she admitted.

Once again she will go into a championship season after tackling the cross country circuit and she will aim to sharpen her speed with altitude training trips to the French Pyrenees. The heat and pollution of the Greek capital city will pose further problems but Radcliffe is more than ready for the challenge.

HELP SOMEONE ELSE ACHIEVE THEIR PERSONAL BEST IN THIS YEAR'S LONDON MARATHON.

Achieving your personal best can go way beyond running. If you become a sponsored runner for The Children's Society, every step you take will help a needy child. Every mile you run, will provide counselling, housing, training and advice. And the moment you cross the finishing line, a lot of young lives will start afresh.

Call Angela Bowen or send off, for a sponsorship pack today, and make your achievement in this year's Marathon, the achievement of a lifetime.

CALL 0171 837 4299.   supported by **SEEBOARD**

For your sponsorship pack, free running vest and baseball cap please contact: Angela Bowen, The Children's Society, Edward Rudolf House, Margery St, London WC1X 0JL

Please tick vest size   ☐ M   ☐ L   ☐ XL

name

address

postcode

tel

The Children's Society
A Voluntary Society of the Church of England and the Church in Wales

Charity Registration No. 221124

Photograph posed by model from Truly Scrumptious, photograph by Steve Shott.

the EGYPTIAN experience

the EGYPTIAN experience

THE CHILDREN'S SOCIETY CYCLE CHALLENGE

Abu Simbel – Luxor

Join us for the Egyptian Experience of a lifetime!

Imagine yourself cycling through the heart of ancient Egypt – the land of the Pharaohs. Spend days enjoying glorious sunshine as you ride through deserts, along the great river Nile to the tombs of the Egyptian kings. Spend nights aboard a Nile Cruiser and under canvas beneath vast star-studded skies as you enjoy traditional food and good company.

The Children's Society have joined together with Classic Tours to offer you a unique opportunity for the bike adventure of a lifetime. And by raising money for The Children's Society, you can be certain that you will be making a real contribution towards helping some of the UK's most vulnerable children.

The eight day cycling challenge from 21 February – 1 March 1998 takes you from the Sun Temple of Abu Simbel to the Great Temples of Luxor. Along the way, you will pass through the desert bordering the Sudan to the Great Dam at Aswan, before continuing beside the River Nile to the Valley of the Kings and Queens – an experience to savour for years to come.

For more information ring the Egyptian Experience hotline:

0171 278 5769

Or write to: The Egyptian Experience, The Children's Society, Edward Rudolf House, Margery Street, London WC1X 0JL.
E-mail: mrv@childsoc.demon.co.uk

Photo: Peter Spurrier

Everyday The Children's Society faces the challenge of helping thousands of the UK's most vulnerable children and young people. Now you have a unique opportunity to help The Children's Society by taking on a tough personal challenge. The Egyptian Experience is a 530 km long bike ride from the Sun Temple of Abu Simbel, through the desert to the Great Dam at Aswan, finishing along the River Nile and the Valley of the Kings and Queens at Luxor. Please take part in what will be a stunning journey to test your endurance and raise much needed funds for the vital work of The Children's Society. The trip and your efforts will not be forgotten!

Matthew Pinsent MBE – Double Olympic Gold Medallist Rower

o: Mao/Gamma

The Children's Society
MAKING LIVES WORTH LIVING
A VOLUNTARY SOCIETY OF THE CHURCH OF ENGLAND
AND THE CHURCH IN WALES
Charity Registration No. 221124

GOOD EVANS: BRITISH MARATHON RUNNING SHOWS ITS HEALTHY SIDE

The marathon boom may be over and the average runner may be getting older – and thus slightly slower – but the UK road race scene is still in a healthy state at both the élite and grass roots end of the sport. STEVE SMYTHE, of 'Runner's World', reports on a year which saw Paul Evans run the third fastest time ever by a Briton

THE first Sunday in December is usually a time of year that only the most committed runner exercises his competitive streak especially as it was a cold and overcast day.

Yet the Victory 5 in Portsmouth had a 1000-strong field. The quality was such that over 30 women broke the

CAPITAL SHOW ... Paul Evans (No8) was beaten in London by Dionicio Ceron (No1)

half-hour and yet leading lady Zara Hyde, who ran the fastest leg in the National Women's Relays, found 140 men in front of her. Further North on the same day, the Leeds Abbey Dash had over 1600 entries even though just 30 miles away the Percy Pud 10K in Sheffield easily reached its 1000 limit and had to turn 300 entries away.

Those numbers may be modest compared to the 25,000 plus taking part in road running's flagships, the London Marathon and Great North Run, but they all showed a high upward trend which is indicative of a thriving sport which has more to it than just two mass events.

For instance, some of the smaller marathons reported record entries while, after a ten-year gap, the Manchester Marathon made a welcome return and attracted well over 2000 runners. Women's running also looks in a healthy state with the Race for Life 5K Series attracting 12,000 women to the 13 races, which was such a success there will be 19 additional race venues in 1997.

While there are certainly concerns about the rising costs of staging events, occasional police interference and a fixture congestion, the backbone of the sport is strong and it's also been a good year for the élite.

Big city wins

There may have been no Olympic medals but there were big city marathon wins for Paul Evans, Liz McColgan and Marian Sutton, international wins for Jon Brown and Paula Radcliffe and a brave Olympic effort from Richard Nerurkar. There were also good marathons from Jon Solly who

as second in Turin (2:12:25) while ...ale Rixon improved to 2:13:41 in fin-...hing fourth (just six seconds behind ...e winner) in Hauts de Seine.

Evans' performance was the most ...otable. Though 35 years old and ...aving been in the top three at New ...ork and London in his two previous ...6 milers, he hadn't quite fulfilled his ...otential until last October. He had ...ever won a marathon and his best ...me until Chicago was outside 2:10.

That changed with his run in the ...Vindy City, which firmly put him ...mongst the world's élite. Three sub-...:50 miles after 18 miles left him clear ...f the field and, maintaining a fast pace ...o the finish, he won by over a minute. ...lis sparkling 2:08:52 made him the ...hird fastest ever Briton and hopefully ...ighly embarrassed the New York City ...narathon organisers who could find no ...oom for him in their budget, despite ...is close second in 1995.

Evans didn't produce the only good ...nen's performance at Chicago as ...amonn Martin, who had earlier won ...ne BAF 10K title in Birmingham, fin-...hed fourth in 2:11:21. While Staines, ...vho won the Great South Run in a ...ast 46:57, was close behind in fifth ...:11:25).

Staines thus improved on his ninth ...t London (2:12:54) where he was in ...ne winning BAF Championship team ...long with his Belgrave clubmate ...vans.

Evans, who won BAF titles at ...narathon and half-marathon with his ...hird at London and his second in the ...reat North Run, turned down selec-...on for the Olympic marathon to con-...entrate on the 10,000m, but there ...vas still a gutsy British performance.

Gutsy performance

Despite stomach problems, Richard ...Jerurkar was a fighting fifth in Atlanta ...n a fine 2:13:39. Though otherwise ...e raced sparingly he clocked a 61:06 ...alf-marathon in Paris. He also ran the ...astest legs in both the National Six-...tage and 12-Stage Relays, enabling ...Bingley to win both events comfortably.

Fellow Olympian Steve Brace strug-...gled in Atlanta, finishing sixtieth, but ...ad earlier run a 2:10:35 marathon in ...nishing a close second at the ...Houston Marathon and after a knee ...operation late in the year may have ...un his last international race.

Peter Whitehead, the revelation of the 1995 World Championships Marathon where he was fourth, had a few good American results including a 28:07 in the Peachtree 10K, but was a disappointing fifty-fifth in Atlanta.

Most of Jon Brown's road race appearances were also in the States and the pick of them was a British record 42:42 in the Gasparilla Classic 15K in Florida where a sub-14-minute last 5K left many of the world's top road runners in his wake.

RUN TALL . . . Marian Sutton won in Chicago

Liz McColgan, who finished second in Florida, has long had a reputation as a renowned front runner but she won Britain's two biggest races by coming from behind. At the London Marathon she was two minutes down on the leader Trine Hakenstad but a succession of 5:30 miles meant the Scot caught the Norwegian at 21 miles to achieve her second fastest ever time of 2:27:54 and her first marathon win for four years .

On that form an Olympic medal looked highly likely but Atlanta was a disappointment for the Scot as an insect bite poisoned her system and held her back to sixteenth. She showed better form at the Great North Run when running down Esther Kiplagat of Kenya in the last 400m to win in a useful 70:28. Her later results weren't to the same standard and she finished her year with a third in the Tokyo Marathon, though her 2:30:50 timing at least put her ahead of Olympic champion Fatuma Roba.

McColgan's Atlanta colleagues also had slightly disappointing seasons after

encouraging starts. Karen Macleod ran a personal best 2:33:50 in Sacramento but injury hampered her Olympic run where she was forty-fifth. Likewise, Suzanne Rigg showed very good form over the half-marathon winning the AAA of England title at Worcester (73:04) and going even quicker at Wilmslow (72:32) but was a below-par cramp-affected fifty-eighth in Atlanta.

Sutton proves her point

Marian Sutton was incensed at being overlooked for Olympic selection but wasn't helped by her modest form fol-lowing a quick Chicago Marathon run towards the end of 1995. She proved her point rather belatedly with excel-lent form in the autumn including a sub-53-minute run in the Great South Run followed by an even better con-trolled piece of running in the 1996 version of Chicago. There she took the lead in the closing miles and improved her pb from the previous year's race to 2:30:41.

Another big British win on American soil came in New York but over the mile rather than the marathon, when Paula Radcliffe front ran to victory in the Fifth Avenue Mile. Her time was a fast 4:26.69.

Radcliffe's former track rival, Yvonne Murray, concentrated on the roads with mixed successes winning the Great Caledonian 10K, but showed a lack of stamina in both the Great North and Great South Runs, which must put a question mark over any future marathon plans.

Over even longer distances, Britain's women enjoyed success. Carolyn Hunter-Rowe won the European 100K title and the team finished third, and they were second in the European 24 Hours Championships with Eleanor Robinson third.

MASSED RANKS . . . The London Marathon was again a great success

WHAT MAKES LIZ McCOLGAN RUN?

In a career which has embraced both euphoric highs and desperate lows, Liz McColgan has won a special place in the hearts of British athletics fans. TOM KNIGHT, the athletics correspondent of *Scotland on Sunday*, discovers what the future holds for her

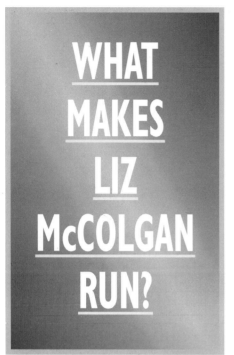

LIZ McCOLGAN will never thrill crowds with an electric turn of speed off the final bend or play to the gallery by toying with opponents but she remains the runners' runner. Her ungainly running action, all thrashing arms and legs, may lack style and grace but her do-or-die attitude to racing has made her a star.

Her celebrated victory over 10,000m at the 1991 World Championships in Tokyo epitomised the very best of Liz McColgan. It was duly described by BBC TV commentator Brendan Foster, himself a former people's favourite on the track, as the greatest long distance run by any British athlete. By the end of that year Liz was a household name, voted BBC Sports Personality of the Year and looking ahead to a golden future as a high-earning marathon runner.

And yet, just over two years ago, that future looked in doubt as a succession of injuries to her back, hamstring, knee and toe threatened to bring her brilliant career shuddering to a halt. For 18 months she struggled to combat the problems and at one stage even had to confront the possibility that she would never run again.

Phenomenal woman

But run again she did. With the doubters still writing her off, she strode to a famous win at last year's London Marathon to prove, yet again, that there was still more to come from this phenomenal woman.

Liz has always embodied the special blend of determination and talent that sets great athletes apart from the rest. In a top-class career going back some 17 years, her gutsy performances on every type of surface have proved inspirational to fans the world over. As well as that world title on the track

she's won two Commonwealth golds and an Olympic silver medal at 10,000m. There's been silver and bronze medals at the World Cross Country Championships and even medals indoors.

When she took to the roads, the rewards kept coming. She won her opening two marathons – the first, in New York, in the fastest ever time for a debutante – and she took the world half-marathon title in 1992. In addition, she's ground out world best times for 10km and the half-marathon.

She appears to have done it all. But one dream remains unfulfilled. The despair she felt in Atlanta, where a severe reaction to an insect bite, of all things, wrecked her hopes of winning an Olympic gold medal in the marathon, might have been enough for most athletes of her standing to call it a day. But the experience only served to stoke up her ambitions still further. Sydney 2000 is the distant target now and she'll keep on running towards the dream.

Now 32 and mother to Eilish, a lively six-year-old, Liz's thoughts do turn to life after athletics. Of course they do. She looks forward to stepping off the treadmill, doing other things and spending more time with husband Peter and Eilish. But all that can wait. Running is everything.

'It's my job and I enjoy what I'm doing,' she said. 'It's as simple as that. I still want to get the best out of myself because I don't think we've seen the best of Liz McColgan yet. I set myself goals and then go all out to achieve them. The goals keep me motivated. I wouldn't keep training the way I do if I wasn't motivated.'

Hot Stuff: McColgan triumphs in Tokyo 91

Golden Moment: McColgan wins in Edinburgh 86

	PROGRESSION AT 10,000M AND MARATHON	
	10,000m	Marathon
1985	33:19.14	-
1986	31:41.42	-
1987	31:19.82	-
1988	31:06.99	-
1989	-	-
1990	32:23.56	-
1991	30:57.07 (UK rec)	2:27:32
1992	31:26.11	2:27:38
1993	-	2:29:37
1994	-	-
1995	31:40.14	2:30:32
1996	-	2:27:54

- Born: May 24th, 1964, Dundee
- Club: Dundee Hawkhill Harriers
- Gold medallist, 1991 World Championships 10,000m
- World champion half-marathon, 1992
- Winner 1991 New York City Marathon and 1996 London Marathon
- 1988 Olympic silver medallist 10,000m
- Commonwealth 10,000m champion 1986 and 1990

Early bird

The training, modified though it may have been when former world champion Grete Waitz became her coach in 1995, remains vigorous and punishing. A self-confessed 'morning person', Liz is invariably in bed before nine and rises before dawn every day to put in the 115 miles a week she clocks up on the roads around her coastal home in Carnoustie.

'I've been getting up at 5.30am for as long as I can remember. It's the time of the day I like best because my energy levels are at their highest then. Sometimes it's hard but as soon as I've got my gear on and I've been running for a couple of minutes, I'm OK. It feels as if I've got the whole world to myself and I'm at one with nature. It's a wonderful feeling.

'I notice things around me but mostly I'm in tune with my body when I'm running. I note how my legs are feeling and I listen to my breathing. Sometimes I'll mentally rehearse racing situations. An athlete always knows how their body is performing because they are aware of how everything should feel when things are going well. I know my own body so well that I can see things in other athletes during races'.

'I knew, for instance, that Yvonne Murray was going to fall apart after six miles of the Great North Run last year. I was watching her closely and I could see that the bounce had gone from her stride.'

One of Waitz's more significant coaching achievements has been in convincing Liz that her previous training, in which 145 miles a week was the norm, was self-destructive. Indeed, the years of such intensive pounding probably caused the injuries which came so close to finishing her off.

'I used to feel guilty if I didn't run some days,' says Liz. 'But Grete got me out of that. You can't just keep flogging yourself like I did because the body won't take it.'

'Stuff You'

The memory of life without running is a constant reminder of that valuable lesson. One medical specialist told her that her career was over and Liz responded with characteristic defiance. 'I just thought: "Stuff you. In your opinion I won't, but in my opinion I will." It was as if what he was saying wouldn't register. It was stubbornness on my part but deep down in my heart I knew I would run again'.

Even so, for three months, after surgery on her knee in 1994, she couldn't exercise at all and took her frustration out on friends and family. Withdrawn and moody, she put on weight and even started drinking to fill the time. All motivation had gone and Liz felt wracked with self-pity.

'I always remember the first time I was able to jog without pain. That was when I knew that I would get back and I felt as good then as I did after winning the World Championship in Tokyo.'

As soon as she was running again, the goals were put in place and it was business as usual, right down to the highs and lows. A lasting problem with a toe joint means that her track races are limited but she still managed to improve her personal best over 5000m in the summer of 1995. The injury will be with her until she has an operation to cure it. Until then, she's content to 'manage' the pain in her own way.

Liz's Olympic year was typical. Victory in London was followed by disaster in Atlanta but she bounced back with a thrilling win in the Great North Run, only to see her form evaporate in Majorca where a niggling strain forced her to pull out of the World Half-Marathon Championship in September – the first time she failed to finish a race. Undeterred, she went straight back into training for the Tokyo Marathon in November.

Best yet to come

She looks forward to living a 'normal life' in which running will be merely for exercise. 'I look forward to leading a normal, active life with less travelling and the time to do all the things I've not been able to do because of my running. I'll always keep fit but instead of being so intense, I'll enjoy other forms of exercise.' And she'll know when to quit the big-time. 'I'll know when to stop,' she says.

Capital Woman: McColgan gets that winning feeling in London

'When I believe I can't win races, I'll step out of it all. I'm not the type to be happy finishing tenth.'

The end of the road may be in sight but there's more to do before she reaches journey's end. 'I know I can run faster and that I haven't reached my best yet. There are still goals to be attained. I now know just how hard it is to win an Olympic gold medal but I'll keep working hard towards it. The next three years are the important ones and there's loads I still want to achieve before I finish with my athletics.'

TRACK GOES TO THE MOVIES

Apart from *Chariots of Fire*, there have not been many memorable movies about athletics. But, as STEVEN DOWNES reports, the balance could be about to be redressed with two films this year about the American runner Steve Prefontaine

LIGHTS, camera, action: its a phrase that ought to be as familiar to athletics as take your marks, set... But although movie makers have turned to athletics for inspiration regularly during the first century of the cinema, only one film based in the sport has ever managed to come up with the cinematic equivalent of a gold medal.

The wafting, willowy notes of Vangelis's soundtrack, laid over slow-motion shots of the group of runners, all splattered with water and sand as they train along the seashore, have become the stuff of cine-clichés in the 15 years since Hugh Hudson's *Chariots of Fire* was released.

Sepia-tinted

In retrospect, although a multiple Oscar-winner, *Chariots* never received great critical acclaim. Criticised for being overly sentimental to the point of seeming sepia-tinted, *Chariots* contained enough lingering period references to make it a sort of Merchant-Ivory in running spikes. That was enough to give it a quaint appeal for American audiences. In this country, the film captured the public mood and imagination of the time – it was released in Britain within weeks of the awe-inspiring first London Marathon.

Where *Chariots* got things most right, however, was that it possessed two elements essential for a commercially successful movie. It had both a dramatic engine for the plot, and a human interest which grabbed and sustained the audience's attention.

In its story of the build-up to the 1924 Olympics for British sprinters Harold Abrahams and Eric Liddell the film had plenty of human interest: there was Abrahams' battle against Establishment anti-semitism and Liddell's strict adherence to his Protestant principles. The dramatic tension and pace was provided, naturally enough, by the fundamental fascination that is contained within any sporting competition.

The essential drama of live sport, after all, is what kept millions of us glued to our television sets during the course of the Atlanta Olympic Games. The only surprise is that, in those shared first 100 years of movie making and the Olympics, so few films have managed to harness the sort of human drama which is so commonly found on the track.

Film makers have turned to baseball and boxing with regular, if variable, success, using those sports as star vehicles. Robert Redford starred in *The*

Natural, Kevin Costner in *Field of Dreams*, Madonna tried to act in *League of their Own*, while Robert de Niro was a *Raging Bull* and Sylvester Stallone made a career out of being *Rocky*. Obviously, America's dominance of the movie industry dictates what films get made – baseball has received wide attention from movie makers, while cricket has been all but ignored; football's laughably small *œuvre* includes *The Highbury Stadium Mystery* and *Escape to Victory*.

Life and (track) times of Prefontaine
Thus, it may be that America's somewhat patronising attitude towards an amateur sport such as track may have stopped there being more films being made with an athletics theme, but this year the balance is due to be redressed, at least a little.

The race to be first to release a movie about the life and (track) times of Steve Prefontaine has been as fiercely fought as some of the contests which he himself once ran. Pre, the 1972 Olympic 5000m fourth placer (beaten to the line by Britain's Ian Stewart), died in a car accident, aged 24, in 1975, and the tales about this fast-running, fast-living athlete have since made him the stuff of legend in Eugene.

That this small, running-mad city in Oregon also happens to be the global headquarters for sportswear company Nike may have also helped in the legend-making process. Prefontaine was one of the first athletes to openly admit to receiving payments for wearing a particular brand of running shoe, and Nike have respected his loyalty to them ever since by maintaining memories of him.

When, two years ago, there were elaborate celebrations of the runner's life, 20 years after his death, including an hour-long television documentary, the idea of making a movie about the running folk hero's life was catapulted to the head of two studios production schedules.

Filming for both projects began last June, although some crowd scenes had already been shot at Hayward Field, the scene of some of Pre's greatest races, the previous month when the Prefontaine Classic Grand Prix event was staged there. Although Disney and Warner had big plans for a big name star to play Pre, Tom Cruise turned down Warner's $15 million project, which will now star Billy Crudup,

while Disney's Prefontaine will be played by Jared Leto, rather than the first-choice Brad Pitt.

The lack of the star name, while an obvious blow to the Pre film's box office potential, need not damage the movie's athletic credibility. After all,

Steve Prefontaine

anyone who remembers seeing *The Games* – a 1960s British-made film directed by Michael Winner about the struggle to win an Olympic marathon – will attest that no matter how well-schooled actors may be, they cannot always convincingly portray an eyeballs-out athlete.

Laughs of derision
In *The Games*, Michael Crawford was the brave Brit – a sort of Jim Peters-style gallant failure who suffered the torture of being coached by psychotic Stanley Baker. He passed athletic muster reasonably well (it is said that in preparing for the role, Crawford managed to run a sub-two-minute 800m), but the acting on the hoof of Ryan O'Neal as the pill-popping American was not convincing, while the casting of Charles Aznavour as an Emil Zatopek character added only one thing to the film: laughs of derision.

However, those of the set of the Warner movie about Prefontaine and who have have seen Crudup's running scenes suggest that this actor seems to have grasped his role well, and with the assistance of Kenny Moore – the former Olympic athlete-turned-sports-writer – as adviser to the movie, then perhaps the portrayals will do justice to the source material.

That was not the case the last time Moore appeared on the big screen. Back in 1982, Moore appeared as a water polo player in Warner's *Personal Best*, who became emotionally and physically involved with Mariel Hemingway, playing a pentathlete preparing for the Olympics. Faux lesbianism in the locker room and other unconvincing portrayals rendered this another sporting cringe-maker.

Graduate with honours
But then, too many movies made about track and field have been strong on bodies, weak on plots. As compelling as the Olympics can be, most of the films that have had athletics as a theme have been bland, or worse, plain comical. Take *It Happened in Athens*, a 1960 film in which the champion of the 1896 Olympic marathon is promised booty far beyond a mere gold medal: he gets to marry Jayne Mansfield.

Nor has the Johnny Weissmuller School of Olympian Acting often seen its pupils graduate with honours. When Bob Mathias played himself in the 1954 bio-pic (imaginatively titled *The Bob Mathias Story*), he was described by the *New York Times* critic as 'as handsome as any young Hollywood idol and twice as guileless in his emoting'.

Like *Chariots of Fire*, *Running Brave* (1983) concentrates on an Olympic title won against adversity at home, with Robby Benson playing Billy Mills, the half-Sioux runner who won the 1964 Olympic 10,000m, and gets closest to producing a film which the viewer can associate and empathise with.

Beautification
That, in part at least, may owe something to the archive documentary footage made of the Tokyo Olympics, which the director and stars of *Running Brave* studied endlessly in order to re-create the race sequences in their film as believably as possible.

In his book about the 1936 Games, *The Nazi Olympics*, Richard D Mandell describes Riefenstahl's film *Olympia*: 'One almost feels a visceral revulsion that the beautification of something so awful should be so successful.' For many drew comparisons between Riefenstahl's Olympic work and an earlier film of Hitler's Nuremburg rallies. Yet despite the hefty stain of its part in Nazi propaganda, *Olympia* is still considered by many to be the greatest sports film ever made, and Riefenstahl the greatest female director.

Four years before Berlin, the Games had been staged in Los Angeles, yet despite being in Hollywood's backyard, the film coverage of those Olympics is minimal. Riefenstahl transformed the way sporting events were filmed. She used a crew of 160, operating 34 cameras. She also ordered and designed radical new equipment: special night filters and telephoto lenses, and the first catapult camera that ran on tracks alongside the sprinters. She had special portable camera towers put up, and she also filmed from balloons and the Graf Zeppelin.

The Olympics as we know them today, with the burning torch, were created in Berlin just over half a century ago, and it was Riefenstahl who captured that image. The IOC was so enraptured with its first official film of the Games that it voted Riefenstahl a gold medal, just like the champions she had immortalised. Her acclaim was capped at the 1938 Venice Film Festival, where Riefenstahl was presented with the award for the year's finest film, beating Disney's *Snow White*. Riefenstahl's version of the Olympics was officially deemed to be better than the stuff of fairy tales.

Fairy story

There was a touch of fairy story, too, about the manner in which Riefenstahl was finally welcomed back after nearly four decades of being ostracised because of her links, real or imagined, with Hitler's Nazi regime. In 1972, despite being originally denied accreditation because of her past Riefenstahl attended the Munich Olympics as a stills photographer. One day during the Games, she attended the premiere of a film about the great hero of the previous Games staged in Germany, Jesse Owens.

Whenever Owens's great Olympian feats are shown today, the programme makers use clips from Riefenstahl's *Olympia*. If Owens's achievements of four gold medals in Berlin are what we know best of those Nazi Games, Riefenstahl is the reason for that understanding.

After the Owens film had finished that day in Munich, amid all the backslapping congratulations, Owens himself stood and, after thanking the producers and directors, he said, 'There is another lady here who is important in my life.' And he pointed to Riefenstahl, sitting at the back of the big room and called her to come up and join him.

Humanity of sport

What Riefenstahl understood was that there is enough drama in sport itself that it rarely needs dramatisation to be created around it. It is a lesson which someone else in that Munich cinema that day also learned. For

Bud Greenspan has been the official film-maker of every Olympics since 1984, using the very humanity of sport to create its own drama to great effect. The director of *Marathon Man*, John Schlesinger, frequently inter-cuts his films chase sequences with archive of Abebe Bikila from Tokyo in 1964, which helps to build the mounting tension of this thriller. William Goldman, himself an occasional runner who adapted his own novel for the screenplay, tells the story of how Dustin Hoffman, when cast to play Babe Levy, was nervous about playing a role of a hardened marathon runner some 15 years younger than his own age. Goldman suggested that Hoffman should watch footage of Frank Shorter winning the Olympic Marathon title in 1972 in Munich; Hoffman, renowned for his preparation for movie roles, went out and met Shorter and got him to pen training schedules for him.

Now, with Pre, the movies are returning to Munich for inspiration. For British athletics sake, at least, let's hope that they do not rewrite history to give the film a happy ending with Prefontaine winning the bronze medal.

Frank Shorter

WHY STAR NAMES AREN'T ALWAYS BEST

FILMS about athletics have often been given the star treatment, but rarely have they benefited.

The 1960 comedy, *Walk, Don't Run*, was set around the 50km walk at the Olympics, and has Cary Grant strolling alongside the racers muttering, 'This is the most ridiculous race,' perhaps thinking that his role in the film is equally absurd.

Jim Thorpe – All American, made in 1951, featured former circus acrobat Burt Lancaster as the first winner of an Olympic decathlon. It is an exchange in this movie which possibly has since been attributed to Thorpe himself. For after presenting Lancaster with his gold medal, the Swedish king says, 'Sir, you are the greatest athlete in the world', which receives the fabulously Hollywood reply of 'Thank you, king.'

Glorious relic

One glorious relic of the British film industry of the 1950s, if you can find it, is a gem called *Wee Geordie*, about a giant Scotsman with immense strength who is discovered just in time for his talents to be geared to throwing the hammer at the 1956 Melbourne Olympics. Bill Travers plays the title role – inevitably, the powers-that-be do not have a team blazer to fit him – though close study of the film fails to reveal which other characters are modelled on Derek Johnson, Mike Farrell or Chris Brasher.

It is not only *Chariots of Fire* among athletic films which has won industry awards. *Babe* (1975), in which Susan Clark played Babe Didrikson, won an Emmy, while in Britain Tom Courtenay received widespread acclaim and helped coin a new expression for the language in *Loneliness of the Long-distance Runner*, a film which pushes *Marathon Man* close as the best melding together of athletic fact and screenwriter fantasy.

Marathon Man also had the benefit of the talents of a stage peer, with Laurence Olivier playing the menacing old Nazi who stalks Dustin Hoffman: do not see this movie if you are due to visit the dentist in the near future.

A number of former athletes, too, have taken to acting, though rarely with great effect. Jim Thorpe himself appeared in movies, as have other multi-eventers Rafer Johnson (alongside Frank Sinatra in *None But The Brave*), Bob Mathias (who gave up acting to go into politics), and Bruce Jenner, who spent several seasons on TV's *CHiPs*.

Former sprinter Bill Cosby, having made his fortune in movies and from being the world's highest paid television performer, at least reinvested some of his fortune in his favourite sport by personally sponsoring the Penn Relays for several years.

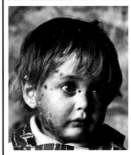

PART FIVE

STATISTICS

UK RANKINGS (MEN) 1996

Key: w=windy; A=altitude; i=indoor; +=set during 1500m

100m

10.00w	Linford Christie (TVH)
10.00	
10.03	
10.13	Darren Braithwaite (Har)
10.17	Darren Campbell (Sale)
10.17	Ian Mackie (Pit)
10.25w	Jason John (Bir)
10.30	
10.26w	Doug Turner (Card)
10.30w	Owusu Dako (Sale)
10.35	
10.30	Adrian Patrick (WSE)
10.38	
10.32w	Michael Rosswess (Bir)
10.38	
10.33w	Allyn Condon (Sale)
10.36	

200m

20.25w	Linford Christie (TVH)
20.29	
20.33A	John Regis (Bel)
20.43	Doug Turner (Card)
20.5w	Roger Black (Team S)
20.56	
20.58	Owusu Dako (Sale)
20.60A	Darren Braithwaite
21.02	
20.6w	Mark Richardson (WSE)
20.85	
20.64	Solomon Wariso (Har)
20.64w	Allyn Condon (Sale)
20.84	
20.67	Doug Walker (NEB)

400m

44.37	Roger Black (Team S)
44.52	Mark Richardson (WSE)
44.57	Jamie Baulch (Card)
44.66A	Iwan Thomas (NEB)
44.69	
44.66	Du'aine Ladejo (Bel)
45.57	Mark Hylton (WSE)
45.66	David Grindley (Wig)
45.76	Guy Bullock (Wig)
46.02	Jared Deacon (Morp)
46.06	Adrian Patrick (WSE)

800m

1:45.69	Craig Winrow (Wig)
1:45.73	Curtis Robb (Liv/Sheff U)
1:45.81	David Strang (Har)
1:46.57	Andy Hart (Cov)
1:47.27	Tom Lerwill (Bel)
1:47.70	Terry West (Morp)
1:47.7	Robin Hooton (CoE/Bris U)
1:47.8	Tony Whiteman (GEC/WLIHE)
1:47.83	Andrew Lill (NEB)
1:47.9	Rupert Walters (Sale/MUAC)

1000m

2:18.48	John Mayock (C&S)
2:18.78	Andy Hart (Cov)
2:18.8i	Tony Whiteman (GEC/WLIHE)
2:19.61	Robin Hooton (CoE/Bris U)
2:20.64	Craig Winrow (Wig)

1500m

3:33.38	John Mayock (C&S)
3:34.47	Tony Whiteman (GEC/WLIHE)
3:37.35	Gary Lough (Anna/LSAC)
3:37.90	Kevin McKay (Sale)
3:38.66	Glen Stewart (CoE)
3:38.95	Curtis Robb (Liv/Sheff U)
3:39.1	Neil Caddy (N&P)
3:40.1	Ian Grime (NEB)
3:40.47	Brian Treacy (Anna)
3:40.7	Robert Whalley (Stoke/Staff U)

Mile

3:50.32	John Mayock (C&S)
3:54.87	Tony Whiteman (GEC/WLIHE)
3:55.39	Rob Denmark (Bas)
3:55.84	Neil Caddy (N&P)
3:59.56	Glen Stewart (CoE)
3:59.98	Richard Ashe (Hill)
4:00.0	Gary Lough (Anna/LSAC)
4:00.42	Robert Hough (Sheff)
4:01.1	Ian Gillespie (Bir)
4:01.2	Philip Healy (Ballyd/Bord)

2000m

5:00.91	John Mayock (C&S)
5:02.98	Gary Lough (Anna/LSAC)
5:02.99	Neil Caddy (N&P)
5:04.11	Rob Denmark (Bas)
5:05.3+	John Nuttall (Pres)
5:06.33	

3000m

7:36.40	John Nuttall (Pres)
7:45.45	Rob Denmark (Bas)
7:52.6	Robert Whalley (Stoke/Sheff U)
7:52.9	Robert Hough (Sheff)
7:53.10i	Jon Wild (Sale/Okla St)

5000m

13:17.48	John Nuttall (Pres)
13:20.10	Jon Brown (Sheff)
13:27.00	Keith Cullen (Chelm)
13:31.36	Rob Denmark (Bas)

13:40.68	Ian Gillespie (Bir)
13:43.49	Chris Sweeney (Tip)
13:45.1	Jon Wild (Sale/Okla St)
13:47.40	Paul Evans (Bel)
13:49.74	Spencer Newport (Bhth)
13:50.04	Christian Stephenson (Card)

10,000m
27:59.72	Jon Brown (Sheff)
28:04.2	Ian Robinson (Pres/Iowa)
28:20.80	Rob Denmark (Bas)
28:24.39	Paul Evans (Bel)
28:32.0	Andrew Pearson (Long)
28:37.87	Martin Jones (Horw)
28:44.09	Chris Sweeney (Tip)
28:47.90	Dermot Donnelly (Anna)
28:55.38	Steve Brooks (Bing/Iowa)
29:08.66	Ian Cornford (SB)

Marathon
2:08:25	Paul Evans (Bel)
2:10:35	Steve Brace (Bridge)
2:11:21	Eamonn Martin (Bas)
2:11:25	Gary Staines (Bel)
2:12:25	Jon Solly (HHH)
2:13:39	Richard Nerurkar (Bing)
2:13:41	Dale Rixon (Card)
2:16:19	Mike O'Reilly (Unatt)
2:16:58	Peter Fleming (Racing C)
2:18:55	Bill Foster (Bhth)
2:18:55	Mark Flint (Tel)

110m Hurdles
13.0w	Tony Jarrett (Har)
13.24	
13.13	Colin Jackson (Brec)
13.5w	Neil Owen (Bel)
13.62	
13.5w	Andy Tulloch (Bel)
13.56	
13.61A	Paul Gray (Card)
13.62w	
13.70	
13.90	Ken Campbell (TVH)
14.01	Ross Baillie (VPAAC)
14.03	Brian Taylor (Old G)
14.04	Damien Greaves (NEB)
14.1w	James Archampong (Swan)
14.14w	
14.19	

400m Hurdles
48.79	Jon Ridgeon (Bel)
49.78	Peter Crampton (Spen)
50.05	Lawrence Lynch (Har)
50.16	Paul Thompson (Bir/Idaho)
50.18	Gary Jennings (NEB/LSAC)
50.36	Chris Rawlinson (Bel)
50.52	Paul Hibbert (Bir)
50.85	Noel Levy (Bel)
50.97	David Savage (Sale)

2000m Steeplechase
5:38.6	Spencer Duval (C&S)
5:40.9	Carl Warren (C&S)

5:42.20	Spencer Newport (Bhth)
5:44.47	Stuart Stokes (Bolt)
5:44.53	Mike Jubb (Der)

3000m Steeplechase
8:26.33	Robert Hough (Sheff)
8:28.32	Justin Chaston (Bel)
8:28.93	Keith Cullen (Chelm)
8:36.71	Spencer Duval (C&S)
8:41.54	Mick Hawkins (Bing)
8:43.21	Kevin Nash (AFD)
8:44.26	Matt O'Dowd (Swin)
8:46.51	Spencer Newport (Bhth)
8:48.34	Lee Hurst (Alt)
8:48.60	Dave Lee (Bhth)

High Jump
2.36i	Steve Smith (Liv)
2.35	
2.34i	Dalton Grant (Har)
2.33	
2.26	James Brierley (Tel)
2.23i	Brendan Reilly (Bel)
2.21	Ben Challenger (Charn)
2.20	Colin Bent (SB/RAF)
2.19i	Mike Robbins (Roth)
2.06	
2.15i	Rob Brocklebank (B'burn)
2.15	
2.15i	Andrew Lynch (TVH)
2.15	Geoff Parsons (Tam)

Pole Vault
5.71	Nick Buckfield (Craw)
5.50	Paul Williamson (TVH/Staff U)
5.50	Neil Winter (SB)
5.45	Mike Edwards (Bel)
5.40i	Matt Belsham (Sale)
5.35	
5.30	Ian Tullett (Bel)
5.30	Kevin Hughes (Har)
5.30	Mike Barber (Bir/Staff U)
5.21	Deon Mellor (Roth)
5.20i	Andy Ashurst (Sale)
5.20	

Long Jump
7.97w	Nathan Morgan (Leic)
7.74	
7.86	Darren Ritchie (Sale/Sc Bord)
7.79	Fred Salle (Bel)
7.79w	Steve Phillips (Bir)
7.75	
7.67	Oni Onuorah (SB)
7.60i	Chris Davidson (NEB)
7.54	
7.57	Julian Flynn (Bir)
7.54	Stewart Faulkner (Bir)
7.54w	Barrington Williams (W&B)
7.52i	
7.42	
7.51w	Mark Bushell (Team S)
7.22	

Triple Jump

17.88	Jonathan Edwards (Gate)
17.22w	Francis Agyepong (SB)
17.18	
16.58	Femi Akinsanya (Peter)
16.53	Julian Golley (TVH)
16.38	Tosi Fasinro (Har)
16.36	Onochie Achike (Craw)
15.90	John Herbert (Har)
15.75	Joe Sweeney (WSE)
15.74w	James Peacock (Thurr)
15.24	
15.67	Carl Howard (NEB/Brun U)

Shot

19.67	Mark Proctor (NEB/RAF)
19.62	Shaun Pickering (Har)
19.22	Matt Simson (Thur)
18.85	Lee Newman (Bel)
18.40	Stephen Hayward (Sale/Sc Border)
17.68i	Simon Williams (Enf)
15.78	
17.46	Mark Edwards (Charn/LSAC)
17.41	Jamie Cockburn (Har)
17.30	Carl Myerscough (B&F)
17.21i	Dave Callaway (Har)
16.72	

Discus

62.40	Robert Weir (Bir)
62.32	Glen Smith (SSH)
58.66	Kevin Brown (Bel)
58.04	Simon Williams (Enf)
56.66	Gary Herrington (Rug)
56.46	Paul Reed (Morp)
56.10	Perris Wilkins (Banb)
55.68	Leith Marar (Bel)
54.74	Neville Thompson (SB)
54.42	Lee Newman (Bel)

Hammer

75.10	David Smith (Bel/ERHS)
73.66	Paul Head (NEB)
72.48	Michael Jones (SB/WLHS)
68.62	Peter Vivian (TVH/WLHS)
67.34	John Pearson (Charn/WLHS)
66.88	Shane Peacock (Bir)
66.08	David Smith (NESH)
63.90	William Beauchamp (TVH)
63.54	Stephen Pearson (Sale/NWHS)
63.08	Gareth Cook (S&D/WLHS)

Javelin

87.44	Steve Backley (Camb H)
83.06	Nick Nieland (SB/Bris U)
81.42	Mick Hill (Leeds)
81.06	Colin McKenzie (NEB)
78.54	Mark Roberson (Har)
77.84	Roald Bradstock (Enf)
76.66i	Stuart Faben (Har)
73.70	
74.60	Nigel Bevan (Bel)
72.76	Keith Beard (Leid)
70.38	Stefan Baldwin (Peter)

Decathlon

7857	Simon Shirley (Bel)
7765	Barry Thomas (Sheff)
7573	Brian Taylor (Old G)
7425	Anthony Southward (CoS)
7480	Dean Macey (Old G)
7204	Eric Hollingsworth (Sheff)
7174	Rafer Joseph (Old G)
7150	Stephen Rogers (Liv P)
6910	Billy Jewers (BMH)
6829	Steve Leader (Enf)

20km Walk

1:23:58	Darrell Stone (Steyn)
1:25:40	Steve Partington (Manx)
1:26:15	Chris Maddocks (Ply)
1:28:39	Andy Penn (Cov)
1:29:48	Martin Young (Road)
1:29:50	Chris Cheeseman (Sy WC)
1:33:17	Richard Oldale (Sy WC)
1:33:28	Kevin Walmsley (Manx)
1:34:05	Andy O'Rawe (Send)
1:34:27	Steve Taylor (Manx)

50km Walk

4:18:41	Chris Maddocks (Ply)
4:22:42	Chris Cheeseman (Sy WC)
4:24:01	Graham White (B&H)
4:27:04	Dennis Jackson (Manx)
4:27:22	Gareth Brown (Edin)
4:32:25	Steve Partington (Manx)
4:35:48	Karl Atton (Leic WC)
4:39:01	Alan King (Leic WC)
4:48:01	Chris Berwick (Leic WC)
4:49:01	Jonathan Cocker (Leic WC)

Key: w=windy; A=altitude; i=indoor; +=set during mile; mx = mixed race

100m

11.39	Simmone Jacobs (SB)
11.42	Marcia Richardson (WSE)
11.46	Paula Thomas (Traff)
11.48	Geraldine McLeod (Bir)
11.48w	Angela Thorp (Wig)
11.49	Sophia Smith (Hallam)
11.50	Bev Kinch (Houn)
11.5	Victoria Shipman (Der)
11.87	
11.5w	Katharine Merry(Bir)
11.54	
11.52	Stephanie Douglas (Sale)

200m

22.88	Katharine Merry (Bir)
22.95	Simmone Jacobs (SB)
23.41	Paula Thomas (Traff)
23.46i	Catherine Murphy (SB)
23.47A	
23.52	
23.57w	Tracy Joseph (BMH)
23.72	
23.6w	Sophia Smith (Hallam)
23.80	
23.62i	Melanie Neef (Glas)
24.6	
24.67	
23.62	Donna Fraser (Croy)
23.64A	Geraldine McLeod (Bir)
23.82i	
24.07	
23.7w	Marcia Richardson (WSE)
23.80	

400m

51.29	Phylis Smith (Sale)
51.45	Sally Gunnell (Ex L)
51.58	Donna Fraser (Croy)
52.48	Georgina Oladapo (Houn)
52.50i	Melanie Neef (Glas)
53.23	
52.71	Linda Keough-Staines (BMH)
52.76	Allison Curbishley (EWM)
52.83	Lorraine Hanson (Bir)
53.22	Michelle Pierre (Croy)
53.52	Stephanie Llewellyn (SB)

800m

1:57.84	Kelly Holmes (ESM/Army)
1:59.87	Diane Modahl (Sale)
2:02.12	Sonya Bowyer (Sale/LSAC)
2:02.76	Natalie Tait (WSE)
2:02.83	Lynn Gibson (Ox C)
2:03.52	Vickie Lawrence (B&F)
2:03.77	Hayley Parry (Swan)

2:04.4mx	Michelle Faherty (Sky)
2:05.97	
2:04.63	Vicky Sterne (Bir)
2:04.87	Jeina Mitchell (Croy)

1500m

4:01.13	Kelly Holmes (ESM/Army)
4:08.42+	Paula Radcliffe (Bed)
4:10.7mx	Sonya Bowyer (Sale/LSAC)
4:17.4	
4:11.0	Alison Wyeth (Park)
4:11.57	Sue Parker (Sale)
4:12.32	Lynn Gibson (Ox C)
4:13.40i	Debbie Gunning (And)
4:17.4	
4:13.52	Angela Davies (BMH/LSAC)
4:14.19	Michelle Faherty (Sky)
4:15.68	Shirley Griffiths (Cram)

Mile

4:24.94	Paula Radcliffe (Bed)
4:38.93	Lynn Gibson (Ox C)
4:39.44	Michelle Faherty (Sky)
4:39.90	Sonya Bowyer (Sale/LSAC)
4:40.93	Liz Francis-Thomas (Card)
4:41.20	Jo Davis/Pavey (Bris)
4:44.60	Shirley Griffiths (Cram)
4:44.79	Sarah Salmon (N&P)
4:46.71	Sarah Bull (Der)
4:48.7	Dianne Henaghan (Morp)

3000m

8:37.07	Paula Radcliffe (Bed)
9:04.4	Sarah Bentley (Bir)
9:04.69i	Sonia McGeorge (B&H/LSAC)
9:09.53	
9:05.45i	Alison Wyeth (Park)
9:09.25	
9:11.2mx	Rhona Makepeace (Charn)
9:15.1	
9:11.68	Sue Parker (Sale)
9:19.4	Lucy Elliott (SB)
9:19.6	Amanda Thorpe/Parkinson (Hynd)
9:21.2	Vikki McPherson (Glas/Glas U)
9:22.2	Hayley Haining (Niths/Glas U)

5000m

14:46.76	Paula Radcliffe (Bed)
15:29.04	Sonia McGeorge (B&H/LSAC)
15:37.07	Vicki Vaughan (Pit)
15:48.91	Alison Wyeth (Park)
15:51.55	Jill Hunter (Valli)
15:53.84	Heather Heasman (Horw)
15:56.15	Lucy Elliott (SB)
16:00.0	Andrea Whitcombe (Park)
16:04.12	Zahara Hyde (Havant)
16:06.2mx	Vikki McPherson (Glas)/Glas U

10,000m

33:17.74	Vikki McPherson (Glas/Glas U)
33:21.46	Louise Watson (GEC/LSAC)
33:33.37	Angie Hulley (Leeds)
34:06.25	Amanda Wright (SB)
34:11.76	Angharad Mair (Newp)
34:26.43	Sharon Dixon (Park)
34:28.13	Sally Goldsmith (EWM)
34:30.52	Jo Thompson (Bath C)
34:37.5	Zahara Hyde (Havant)
34:41.28	Mara Myers (Ox U)

Marathon

2:27:54	Liz McColgan (Dund)
2:30:41	Marian Sutton (West)
2:33:50	Karen Macleod (Edin)
2:34:11	Sally Goldsmith (Edin)
2:38:47	Angharad Mair (Newp)
2:38:52	Sally Eastall (St Ed)
2:39:46	Danielle Sanderson (Wat)
2:44:39	Trudi Thompson (Pit)
2:44:49	Tracy Swindell (Thurr)
2:45:12	Gillian Horovitz (AFD)

100m Hurdles

12.80	Angela Thorp (Wig)
13.13w	Diane Allahgreen (Liv)
13.27	
13.18	Denise Lewis (Bir)
13.18	Jacqui Agyepong (SB)
13.23w	Melanie Wilkins (AFD)
13.41	
13.30w	Clova Court (Bir)
13.6	
13.65	
13.3	Michelle Campbell (Ex L)
13.61w	
13.80	
13.38w	Sam Farquharson (Croy)
13.40	
13.39w	Keri Maddox (C&S/Staff U)
13.5	
13.53	
13.59	Jane Hale (Sale)

400m Hurdles

54.65	Sally Gunnell (Ex L)
56.43	Alyson Layzell (Chelt)
56.45	Louise Fraser (Traff)
56.61	Louise Brunning (SUT D/LSAC)
57.03	Lorraine Hanson (Bir)
57.27	Vicki Jamison (Lagan V)
57.78	Gowry Retchakan (Thurr)
58.80	Sinead Dudgeon (EWM)
58.8	Allison Curbishley (EWM)
58.85	Vyvyan Rhodes (Hallam)

High Jump

1.94	Debbie Marti (Brom)
1.92	Lea Haggett (Croy)
1.89	Jo Jennings (Ex L)
1.88i	Julia Bennett (E&E)
1.88	
1.87	Susan Jones (Wig)

1.86i	Michelle Dunkley (Kett)
1.85	
1.85	Rachael Forrest (Bir)
1.84	Denise Lewis (Bir)
1.84	Hazel Melvin (Glas)
1.80i	Kelly Thirkle (Sale)
1.75	

Pole Vault

4.00	Janine Whitlock (Traff)
3.90	Kate Staples (Ex L)
3.70	Rhian Clarke (Ex L)
3.70	Paula Wilson (Bir)
3.60	Linda Stanton (Roth)
3.55	Louise Schramm (E&E)
3.55	Emma Hornby (Bir)
3.51i	Clare Ridgley (Team S)
3.50	
3.50	Fiona Harrison (Barns)
3.30i	Claire Morrison/Adams (Bris)
3.30	

Long Jump

6.66	Denise Lewis (Bir)
6.47A	Ashia Hansen (SB)
6.11	
6.47	Joanne Wise (Cov)
6.34w	Sarah Claxton (C&T)
6.24	
6.22	Debbie Marti (Brom)
6.14	Vikki Schofield (Roth)
6.13	Liz Ghojefa (E&E)
6.13	Tracy Joseph (BMH)
6.10	Ann Brooks (CoH0
6.08	Jade Johnson (HHH)

Triple Jump

14.78	Ashia Hansen (SB)
14.04	Michelle Griffith (WSE)
13.55	Connie Henry (SB)
13.28	Rachel Kirby (Bhth)
13.03	Shani Anderson (SB)
12.72	Mary Agyepong (SB)
12.67	Caroline Stead (Park)
12.61w	Karen Skeggs (Ash)
12.49i	
12.42	
12.58w	Katie Evans (Bir)
12.40	
12.55	Pamela Anderson (Glas)

Shot

19.01	Judy Oakes (Croy)
16.81	Myrtle Augee (Brom)
15.80i	Maggie Lynes (Ex L)
13.89	
15.24	Sharon Andrews (Ex L)
14.76	Tracy Axten (Houn)
14.67	Jo Duncan (Ex L)
14.66	Alison Grey (Glas)
14.60	Philippa Roles (Swan)
14.48	Debbie Callaway (AF&D)
14.43	Emma Beales (Mil K)

Discus

60.04	Jacqui McKernan (Lis/LSAC)
58.56	Debbie Callaway (AF&D)
57.34	Shelley Drew (Sut D)/BUAC
55.88	Tracy Axten (Houn)
52.34	Lorraine Shaw (Sale)
52.10	Sharon Andrews (Ex L)
51.38	Philippa Roles (Swan)
51.24	Nicola Talbot (Tel)
50.70	Emma Beales (Mil K)
49.74	Sarah Henton (Bir/BUAC)

Hammer

61.34	Lorraine Shaw (Sale)
59.54	Lyn Sprules (Houn)
55.00	Ann Gardner (Cor)
53.26	Sarah Moore (Bris)
52.06	Diana Holden (Houn)
50.72	Esther Augee (Ex L)
50.62	Helen Arnold (Port)
50.32	Irene Duffin (SB)
49.80	Samantha Burns-Salmond (Traff)
49.52	Rachael Beverley (Mand)

Javelin

64.06	Tessa Sanderson (Houn)
60.12	Shelley Holroyd (Ex L)
58.20	Lorna Jackson (EWM)
56.50	Denise Lewis (Bir)
56.16	Sharon Gibson (Notts)
54.44	Mandy Liverton (Exe)
53.74	Karen Martin (Der/WRAF)
50.96	Karen Costello (Glas/Heriot U)
50.80	Janine King (Traff)
49.10	Alison Moffitt (N Down)

Heptathlon

6645	Denise Lewis (Bir)
5747w	Julia Bennett (E&E)
5356	
5703	Kerry Jury (Wig)
5700	Vikki Schofield (Roth)
5618w	Sarah Damm (CoS)
5386	Pauline Richards (Bir)
5339	Tracy Joseph (BMH)
5332	Diana Bennett (E&E)
5258	Anne Hollman (Peter)
5213	Nicole Gautier (Hallam)

10km Walk

47:05	Vicky Lupton (Sheff WC)
47:12	Verity Snook (AFD)
48:00	Carolyn Partington (Manx)
48:27	Lisa Langford (W&B)
48:47	Melanie Wright (Nun)
49:37	Karen Kneale (Manx)
50:45	Kim Braznell (Sheff WC)
51:17	Liz Corran (Manx)

LINFORD CHRISTIE
100m & 200m

Thames Valley Harriers.
2.04.60. PB: 60m 6.47i (Eur rec, 95);
100m 9.87 (Eur & Comm rec, 93);
200m 20.09 (88) & 20.25i (World
rec, 95).
Time finally caught up with Christie in
his last year on the international
circuit. After ten years at the top and
already established as Britain's greatest
ever sprinter, he left it until three weeks before the Games
before announcing his participation at his third Olympics. Short
of genuine medal form before leaving for the USA despite
retaining both his European Cup sprint titles and winning his
26th AAA title, he still promised a grand finale in Atlanta. He
clocked his fastest time of the season, 10.03, in the second
round but his defence of the Olympic 100m title ended with
two false starts and automatic disqualification in the final. He
could only watch in disbelief as the gold medal and world
record went to Donovan Bailey, the Canadian who had
snatched his world title 12 months previously. He lasted only
two rounds of the 200m and never even managed a run in the
4x100m because the team dropped the baton in the opening
heat. Christie's proud record of never having been beaten over
100m by another Briton in ten years also went last summer.
Scottish prospect Ian Mackie ended the run at Sheffield on 25
August. He ended his career as Britain's most bemedalled athlete to concentrate on his business career with Nuff Respect,
the management company he represents with Colin Jackson,
and to coach aspiring sprinter, Darren Campbell.

ROGER BLACK 400m

Team Solent. 31.03.66. PB: 44.37
(British rec, 96).
Ten years after bursting on to the
scene, Black enjoyed his greatest triumph in Atlanta when he won the silver medal behind Michael Johnson at
the Centennial Olympic Games. He also anchored Britain's
relay quartet to silver behind the Americans with a last leg
clocked at 43.87. The oldest by far of Britain's outstanding
crop of 400m runners, Black dominated throughout the season. He set a new UK record of 44.39 in winning the AAA
title in June and lowered it to 44.37 in Lausanne the next
month. A 200m pb of 20.56 as early as April heralded what
was to come. Black intends going on to Sydney in 2000
'health and fitness permitting' and recently emerged as a
leading force in the new British Athletes' Association.

CRAIG WINROW 800m

Wigan & District Harriers. 22.12.71. PB: 1:45.69.
An outstanding teenager who has yet to make a major
breakthrough at senior level, Winrow maintained his No 1
ranking with a series of personal bests last summer. Twice
English Schools and AAA champion as a junior, he won the
European Junior title in 1989 in Varazdin at just 17. The following year he won a silver medal in the 4x400m at the
World Juniors. He had to wait until 1994 before making his
senior GB debut in a season in which he won the AAA
Championships and finished third in that year's European
Cup. He was sixth in the European Championship final and
fourth at the Commonwealth Games. He ended his most
successful season by finishing third in the World Cup final at
Crystal Palace. In Atlanta, at his first Olympic Games, he
reached the semi-finals.

JOHN MAYOCK 1500m

Cannock & Stafford. 26.10.70. PB: 3:33.38.
Finished 11th in the Olympic final in Atlanta after coming
through his tough semi-final as a fastest loser but 1996
was a good year for Mayock. He won the AAA title and, in
lowering his personal best to 3:33.38 in Rieti at the end of
the season, established himself as a truly world-class met-
ric miler. He also topped the year's UK rankings at 1000m
(2:18.48), the mile (3:50.32 at the Bislett Games in Oslo)
and 2000m (5:00.91). A Commonwealth Games bronze
medallist from 1994, Mayock is advised by, among others,
Peter Elliott, the 1990 Commonwealth champion. He won
gold over 5000m at the 1991 World Student Games in
Sheffield where he competed as a late replacement, taking
22.16 secs off his personal best in the final. He also won a
3000m silver in the 1992 European Indoors, where he
improved his pb twice; by more than seven seconds in the
heat and by a further four seconds in the final.

JOHN NUTTALL 5000m

Preston Harriers. 11.01.67. PB: 13:16.70.
Topped the UK rankings in 1996 in a year in which he
combined success across the country and on the track. He
secured his Olympic selection by winning the AAA title in
Birmingham, where he beat pre-race favourite Rob
Denmark. In Atlanta, he reached the semi-finals. Earlier in
the year, he won the English National Cross Country title
at Newark by 20 seconds and competed in the World
Cross Country Championships in South Africa. In 1994,

Nuttall was top Briton at the World Cross Country Championships before finishing fifth in the European Championship 5000m in Helsinki and winning a bronze medal at the Commonwealth Games in Victoria.

JON BROWN
10,000m

Sheffield. 27.02.71. PB: 27:59.72. Brown rounded off a great year by becoming the first British man for 21 years to lift a major cross country title when he won the European Championship race in Charleroi, Belgium, in December. During the year he established himself as the UK's top distance runner. In February he won the famous Gasprilla 15km road race in the USA. He finished twelfth, and first European, in the World Cross Country Championships in Cape Town in March. Despite suffering an untimely cold, he acquitted himself well at the Olympics, finishing tenth and second European in the 10,000m final, where he clocked his personal best. He ended the year as the only Briton to run under 28 minutes on the track.

PAUL EVANS
Marathon

Belgrave Harriers. 13.04.61. PB: 2:08:52. Far and away Britain's best marathon runner in 1996 when he at last achieved the major victory he had been promising when he won October's Chicago Marathon in 2:08:52 and became the first Briton to run inside 2:10 for seven years. This, after being denied a place in the line-up for the 1996 New York City Marathon. Six months previously, he finished third in the London Marathon, in 2:10:40, behind Dionicio Ceron and Vincent Rousseau. He still holds the European best for the half-marathon (60:09 in 1995). Having opted out of Olympic marathon selection, he failed to finish the final of the 10,000m in Atlanta.

JUSTIN CHASTON 3000m Steeplechase

Belgrave Harriers. 4.11.68. PB: 8:23.90.
AAA champion for the second time in 1996 when he also achieved the Olympic qualifying time. In Atlanta, he made it to the semi-finals where he finished ninth in his race. The Texas-based student from Cardiff was the Welsh 5000m champion in 1994.

COLIN JACKSON
110m Hurdles

Brecon AC. 18.02.67. PB: 12.91 (World rec, 93). Never really got into his stride in 1996 after getting over the niggling injuries and upsets which had so dogged his 1995 campaign. Achieved his best time of the year, 13.13, in winning the AAA title but had no answer to American world champion, Allen Johnson, in Atlanta. Jackson finished fourth in the Olympic final. He so wanted to erase the memory of finishing seventh at the 1992 Games where he was the odds-on favourite as world No 1. The silver medal he won as a youngster in 1988, in Seoul, is destined to be his best effort. Enjoyed his best years in 1993 and 1994 when he was virtually unbeatable. World champion in 1993 when he broke the world record in Stuttgart, he went through the 1994 season unbeaten and retained both his European and Commonwealth titles at a canter. In 1994 he also achieved a unique double in winning both the 60m and 60m hurdles gold medals at the European Indoor Championships. His winning streak of 44 successive sprint hurdles victories from 29 August, 1993, was ended by Johnson on 9 February, 1995, indoors in Madrid.

JON RIDGEON 400m Hurdles

Belgrave Harriers. 14.02.67. PB: 48.73. Nicknamed 'The Comeback Kid' after his remarkable reappearance on the international scene in 1996 following three seasons out with injury. He had, in fact, 'retired' in 1993 after persistent Achilles tendon problems. But the former sprint hurdler, who won a silver medal at the 1987 World Championships, discovered that his injuries had healed while he pursued a career in sports marketing off the track. Coaching by Mike Whittingham and training with Roger Black during the 1995–96 winter paid off and Ridgeon quickly established himself as British No 1 over 400m hurdles. He won the AAA title in 49.16 and reached the Olympic semi-finals. His pb, however, dates back to the end of the 1992 season when he finished second in the World Cup.

STEVE SMITH
High Jump

Liverpool Harriers. 29.03.73. PB: 2.37 (British rec, 92 & 93).
The world junior champion and record holder from 1992
finished the 1996 season ranked fourth in the world. He
came away from the Olympics in Atlanta with a bronze
medal after clearing 2.35 – his best of the summer – in an
exciting final and has now won medals at all four major
championships. It's yet to be gold at senior level but it surely

won't be long. He first jumped 2.37 in winning the World
Junior gold and managed it again when taking the bronze
medal at the 1993 World Championships, both indoors and
out. His medal in Stuttgart that year was the first outdoors
by a Briton in the men's high jump at world or Olympic
level since 1908.

NICK BUCKFIELD Pole Vault

Crawley AC. 5.06.73. PB: 5.71 (British rec, 96).
Solely responsible for the resurgence in British pole vaulting,
Buckfield first hit the heights in July 1995, when he succeeded Keith Stock as UK record holder after clearing 5.70 in
Sheffield. He improved the record by a single centimetre in
winning last season's AAA and Olympic trials. In Atlanta,
however, he failed to make the final after managing only 5.40
in qualifying.

NATHAN MORGAN Long Jump

Leicester Cor. 30.06.78. PB: 7.74.
Morgan heads the season's rankings after winning the English
Schools title with a wind-assisted 7.97 in July, though his
best legal mark came when he won bronze at the World
Juniors in Sydney. The 6ft 5in youngster goes into 1997 as a
leading hope for the European Junior title although, in an
event bereft of talent at senior level, his services may also be
called upon for this summer's European Cup.

JONATHAN EDWARDS Triple Jump

Gateshead Harriers. 10.05.66. PB: 18.29 (World rec, 95).
Only for Edwards would a silver medal at the Atlanta
Olympics be considered a failure! By leaping into the history
books with the first ever
18-metre triple jump, albeit
windy, at the 1995
European Cup, Edwards
became an overnight sen-
sation. He took Willie
Banks' world record with
17.98 in Salamanca, Spain,
later that summer and
achieved the unpreced-
ed feat of world records
with his first two attempts
at that summer's World
Championships in
Gothenburg – 18.16 and
18.29. They were the first

legal jumps of 18m and 60ft. He remained unbeaten all season and continued his winning ways in 1996, although his
jumping was less spectacular. He ended the season finishing
second overall in the IAAF Grand Prix and with only two
defeats on his record – it just happened that one of them
came in the one competition that mattered. American
Kenny Harrison won the gold in Atlanta.

SHAUN PICKERING Shot

Haringey AC. 14.11.61. PB: 19.62.
Some 18 years after his first English Schools title in the hammer, Pickering achieved a lifetime ambition by competing in
the 1996 Olympic Games. This, after giving up his job some
12 months before to prepare properly. It was while training
in the USA that he improved his pb from 18.94 to 19.62. He
managed only 18.29 in Atlanta and failed to make the final.
He is the son of the former BBC commentator, the late Ron
Pickering, and Jean Desforges, the 1954 European long jump
champion.

ROBERT WEIR Discus

Birchfield Harriers. 4.02.61. PB: 63.56.
Threw in the Atlanta Games – where he failed to qualify for
the final – 12 years after his last appearance in the
Olympics. Back in 1984 he finished tenth in the hammer at
Los Angeles before giving up athletics to concentrate on
American football. A US resident, he took up athletics again
in 1993 and is currently throws coach at Stanford University,
California. Commonwealth hammer champion in 1982, he
returned to that competition again, 12 years later, to win a
bronze medal, in the discus, in 1994. He once set a world
best indoors of 23.64 for throwing the 35lb weight.

DAVE SMITH Hammer

Belgrave Harriers. 2.11.74. PB: 75.10.
Only 21 when he won the AAA Championships and Olympic Trials against far more experienced opposition, Smith was Britain's only hammer thrower in Atlanta. The gentle giant from Grimsby, who stands 6ft 5in, has improved steadily since 1992.

STEVE BACKLEY Javelin

Cambridge Harriers. 12.02.69. PB: 91.46 (British rec, 93).
Backley's Olympic silver medal in Atlanta was all the more remarkable because of his efforts to return after injury earlier in the summer. He started his season late after an operation in the spring but hit form immediately and achieved his season's best of 87.44 with his opening throw in the Olympic final. He won the bronze medal in 1992 and, despite numerous injury problems over the years, he has remained Britain's most consistent performer on the big occasion. Twice the European and Commonwealth champion (1990 and 1994), he has held the world record three times. He threw 89.58 with a Sandvik javelin in Stockholm and 90.98 with a Nemeth model at Crystal Palace, both in 1990 and when that type of javelin was banned at the end of 1991, his original mark was reinstated as the world record. At the start of 1992 he became the first man to throw 90 metres with the revised javelin specification.

BARRY THOMAS Decathlon

Sheffield. 28.04.72. PB: 7661 points. The AAA's champion, he narrowly missed obtaining the standard necessary to be selected for the Atlanta Olympics.

DARRELL STONE 20km Walk

Steyning. 2.02.68. PB: 1:23:27. Britain's best over 20km for several years, he also missed out on Atlanta because he was unable to obtain the qualifying time despite many attempts.

CHRIS MADDOCKS 50km Walk

Plymouth City. 28.03.57. PB: 3:51:37. Competed in his fourth Olympics in Atlanta, where he finished thirty-fourth. The British record holder, his best championship placing was fourth in the 1986 Commonwealth Games 30km.

SIMMONE JACOBS 100m

Shaftesbury Barnet. 5.09.66. PB: 11.31.
A consistent performer for Britain for the last ten years, her greatest success on the international stage has come as part of the sprint relay quartet. She's won silver and bronze medals at the Commonwealth Games (1990 and 1994) and bronze at the 1990 European Championships. She also won a bronze medal at the Los Angeles Olympics in 1984. Surprisingly edged into second place at last summer's AAA, she went to Atlanta, where she was eliminated in the second round of the 100m and 200m and finished eighth with the relay squad in the 4x100m final.

KATHARINE MERRY 200m

Birchfield Harriers. 21.09.74. PB: 22.85.
Injury has hampered her progress but Merry remains one of Britain's brightest prospects over 200m. At just 14 years old, she set world age records at 50 and 100m and went to three European Junior Championships. On the last occasion, in 1993, she won gold medals in the 200m and relay. Her senior career has been faltering out but, in her first Olympics, in Atlanta, she reached the second round of the 200m and appeared in the 4x100m relay.

PHYLIS SMITH 400m

Wigan Harriers. 29.09.65. PB: 50.22. Became an overnight celebrity when she reached the final of the 1992 Barcelona Olympics and was reprimanded by the IOC for writing the name of her local butcher who had given her free meat on her number! Two years later she produced a magnificent run to win the bronze medal in the European Championships in Helsinki. But she then entered a period of injuries which kept her out for nearly two years. She reached the second round in Atlanta and hopes, now she has put her injury problems behind her, she can challenge for a place in the final in Athens. A former nurse, Smith always races in gloves because of poor circulation.

KELLY HOLMES 800m/1500m

Ealing & The Army. 19.04.70. PB: 800m 1:56.21 (British rec, 95) 1500m 4:01.13. Britain's unluckiest athlete in 1996. As a bronze and silver medallist at the 1995 World Championships, she went to Atlanta confident of improving on both at the

Olympics. But, hit by injury while at the training camp in Tallahassee, Florida, she struggled through both events. Her brave run in the 800m earned her fourth place after a frantic sprint down the home straight and, despite pain-killing injections before each race, she still made it to the 1500m final. Again, she tried to defy the odds and take the race to her opponents but ran out of steam and finished eleventh. Up until the Olympics she had enjoyed a fabulous season, becoming the first woman since Diane Leather in 1957 to win an AAA middle-distance double.

PAULA RADCLIFFE 5000m

Bedford & County. 17.12.73.
PB: 14:46.76 (British rec, 96).
An outstanding junior who beat Wang Junxia when she won the 1992 World Junior Cross Country title in Boston. Over the country she has won the English and UK titles and taken her winter form onto the track. Fifth in the 1995 World Championships, she went to Atlanta after achieving a First Class Honours degree in European Studies at Loughborough University. Fifth again in the Olympics, she produced her best form just days later. In one week on the IAAF Grand Prix circuit, she shattered her personal bests for the mile and 3000m and broke Zola Budd's 11-year-old British record for the 5000m.

VIKKI McPHERSON 10,000m

City of Glasgow. 1.06.71. PB: 32:32.42.
Ran in the shadow of Liz McColgan when she first appeared on the national scene and even stepped in for her at short notice when McColgan was unable to run in the 1994 European Cup. She was the Scottish cross country champion in 1993 and 1994 and captained her country's athletics team at the 1994 Commonwealth Games. In the absence of fellow Scot, Yvonne Murray, she topped the 1996 rankings with 33:17.74.

LIZ McCOLGAN Marathon

Dundee Hawkhill Harriers. 24.05.64. PB: 2:27.32.
In many ways, 1996 was a typical year in the life of Liz McColgan, when success was matched by disappointment in equal measures. Finally running well again following her 12-month lay-off with injury (1993–94), she won the London Marathon at her third attempt in April and went to Atlanta

among the favourites for the Olympic gold. But an insect bite just 48 hours before the race turned sceptic and she could finish only sixteenth after overcoming sickness and lack of sleep. Barely a month later she was back to her best to win the Great North Run with a sprint finish along the seafront at South Shields. Later in September she dropped out of the World Half-Marathon Championships in Majorca, troubled by a niggling hamstring. She ended the year by finishing third in the Tokyo Marathon in November, a race she had previously won in 1992. World champion at 10,000m from 1991 – her finest race – and the Olympic silver medallist in 1988, McColgan won her first two marathons, in New York and Tokyo, and still holds the world best for the half-marathon (67:11 in 1992).

ANGIE THORP 100m Hurdles

Wigan AC. 7.12.72. PB: 12.80 (British rec, 96).
Enjoyed a fantastic Olympics, where she reached the semi-finals, finishing fifth and breaking Sally Gunnell's eight-year-old British record with 12.80. Thorp won the AAA title after battling against injury and illness throughout 1994 and 1995. She previously won ten county titles in her native Yorkshire.

SALLY GUNNELL 400m Hurdles

Essex Ladies. 29.07.66. PB: 52.74 (World rec, 93).
Her brave attempt to defend her Olympic 400m hurdles title in Atlanta ended in agony half-way round her semi-final when injury struck. Having missed virtually the whole of the 1995 season with one Achilles needing an operation, it was the other which let her down in 1996. Now she has decided to try one more season on the track in a bid to win back the World Championship crown she claimed in a world record time in 1993. The British women's team captain has enjoyed a fabulous career and has rightly become a house-hold name because of her performances both on and off the track. A former Commonwealth champion over 100m hurdles, Olympic and World relay bronze and held the world 400m hurdles record for two years (1993–95). Regular TV appearances include hosting Carlton's *Body Heat* for ITV.

DEBBIE MARTI High Jump

Bromley Ladies. 14.05.68. PB: 1.94.
Held the world age record for under-15s when she cleared 1.88 in 1983 but could only manage 1.85 in Atlanta when she was eliminated in the qualifying stages of the Olympic competition. She did win her third AAA title in 1996, however, when she jumped a championship best of 1.94 and came close to the UK record of 1.96.

DENISE LEWIS Heptathlon & Long Jump

Birchfield Harriers. 27.08.72. PBs: Heptathlon 6645 points (British rec, 96) Long Jump 6.67.
Voted the British Athletics Writers' Association female athlete of the year after her Olympic bronze medal in the heptathlon – our only female medallist in track and field. The medal had looked a lost cause after the first day of competition when Lewis's performances were below par. But she came back with a bullet in the javelin where a personal best of 54.82 earned her 954 points. Earlier in the year her new personal best points tally broke Judy Simpson's ten-year-old British record when she finished runner-up to Ghada Shouaa of Syria in the International Combined Events competition in Gotzis, Austria. She recorded personal bests in the 100m hurdles (13.18) and shot (14.36). Lewis was the surprise Commonwealth champion in 1994, when she improved her javelin best by more than five metres and took two seconds off her 800m best. She ended the year ranked second in the world behind Shouaa, now the world and Olympic champion. Her long jump best for the season was 6.66. She won the AAA title but failed to make the final in Atlanta.

ASHIA HANSEN Triple Jump

Essex Ladies. 5.12.71. PB: 14.78 (British rec, 96). Born in Indiana in the US and taken to live in Ghana for six years before coming to the UK, Hansen has emerged as Britain's top triple jumper as the event has entered the Olympic timetable. She began the year with a great series of competitions indoors, setting UK and Commonwealth records but she missed out on the medals at the European Indoors. Went to Atlanta after jumping a championship best of 14.25 with her first attempt at the AAA. In the first ever Olympic competition, she finished fourth, before embarking upon a post-Atlanta campaign which saw her regularly break the British record.

JUDY OAKES Shot

Croydon. 14.02.58. PB: 19.38 (British rec, 88).
One of the unsung heroines of the British team, Oakes celebrated her record seventy-fourth appearance in a national vest indoors last winter. In a career stretching back to the late 1970s, she has won medals at all five Commonwealth Games she's contested, including the gold in 1982 in Brisbane and in 1994 in Victoria. She still argues that the bronze medal from the 1984 Olympic Games in Los Angeles should be hers, since Australian Gael Martin's admission that she used performance enhancing drugs. Disillusioned with the sport, she retired in 1991 only to return three years later at the age of 36 to win the Commonwealth title. Last summer, Oakes reached the final in Atlanta – where she finished eleventh – after winning the thirty-seventh AAA gold medal of her career, exceeding the Olympic qualifying standard of 18 metres with all five throws.

JACQUI McKERNAN Discus

Lisburn. 1.07.65. PB: 60.72.
McKernan won her sixth AAA title but was unable to reach the Olympic qualifying standard. Her best international performance came at the 1990 Commonwealth Games in Auckland, where she won the silver medal. She was fifth at the 1994 Games.

TESSA SANDERSON Javelin

Hounslow. 14.03.56. PB: 73.58.
Sanderson provided one of the athletics stories of the year when she decided to make a comeback in 1996 to spearhead a £1 million fund-raising campaign for the Children in Hospital Charity.
Retired for four years – after finishing fourth at the Barcelona Games – the 1984 Olympic gold medallist, three time Commonwealth champion and former British record holder wanted to compete in a record sixth Olympics. Not only did she make it to Atlanta, but she added some much needed glamour and style to the track and field scene in 1996. Her first appearance, at Bedford in May, saw her achieve the Olympic qualifying standard of 60 metres with her first  throw. Her best of the season, 64.04, came in winning the London Grand Prix meet at Crystal Palace on the eve of the Games. Sadly, she never came close to 60 metres in Atlanta and failed to qualify for the final. The good news is that she enjoyed herself so much that she plans to stick around for at least another season.

VICKY LUPTON 10km Walk

Sheffield RWC. 17.04.72. PB: 45:18.
The British No 1 race walker since 1992 finished thirty-third in the Olympic 10km in Atlanta. When she won the 5km event at last summer's AAA Championships, her mother Brenda finished fourth.

Why is the *Minimal Bounce Bra*® and **M.A.N**™ the most important pieces of sports equipment a woman and man can wear?

M.A.N™

The unique STRAPLESS and POUCHLESS design of Dans-ez M.A.N comfortably and most effectively with the help of cotton/Lycra* gives firm, gentle and lasting support.

A revolutionary front construction enhances nature's design of natural retraction occurring in fight or flight situations often simulated in competitive sports.

No unsightly, irritating straps! Specially designed full rear portion comfortably covers buttocks.

Comfortable wide supportive salt resistant waistband - because of Lycra - does not roll or slip. Never loses shape!

Doubled layer sleeve takes protective box. Only natural comfortable absorbent cotton touches the skin allowing it to breathe naturally.

*Lycra is **DUPONT's** registered trade mark for its elastane fibre.

Marketed by - Dans-ez International Ltd., 7 Blenheim Close, Pysons Road Industrial Estate, Broadstairs, Kent. CT10 2YF. Tel: 01843 866300. Fax: 01843 860880

DANS EZ® Minimal Bounce Bra®

The original and best

Dans-ez Minimal Bounce Bra, because of its unique CUPLESS design and special blend of cotton/Lycra*, comfortably and very effectively minimises painful breast bounce and the accompanying irreversible stretching of Cooper's Ligaments and equally painful nipple soreness.

The specially designed midriff portion never rides up causing discomfort and irritation.

Amazingly no hooks, clasps or wires! No irritating seams, darts or hardware!

Dans-ez Minimal Bounce Bra's shoulder straps and low back are designed to be worn without showing under most sleeveless leotards and sports tops.

NO NYLON! Nylon increases perspiration and can cause potential skin irritation.

Only natural, soft comfy absorbent cotton touches your skin, allowing it to breathe naturally.

Dans-ez Minimal Bounce Bra – it's exactly what you have always wanted. You'll love it.

Dans-ez is a registered trade mark.

Matching thong or full briefs £13.99 inc. p.&p. (phone for details)

OLYMPIC GAMES

Centennial Stadium, Atlanta, 26 July – 4 August 1996

MEN

100m (+0.7):

1	Donovan Bailey CAN	9.84 WR
2	Frankie Fredericks NAM	9.89
3	Ato Boldon TRI	9.90
4	Dennis Mitchell USA	9.99
5	Mike Marsh USA	10.00
6	Davidson Ezinwa NIG	10.14
7	Michael Green JAM	10.16

LINFORD CHRISTIE GBR dsq

GB: Ian Mackie dns SF (injured) 2rh5 3		10.25
Darren Braithwaite 2rh3 6		10.27

200m (+0.4):

1	Michael Johnson USA	19.32 WR
2	Frankie Fredericks NAM	19.68
3	Ato Boldon TRI	19.80
4	Obadele Thompson BAR	20.14
5	Jeff Williams USA	20.17
6	Ivan Garcia CUB	20.21
7	Patrick Stevens BEL	20.27
8	Mike Marsh USA	20.48
GB: John Regis SFh1 6		20.58
Linford Christie 2rh2 4		20.59
Owusu Dako 1rh2 4		20.83

400m:

1	Michael Johnson USA	43.49 OR
2	ROGER BLACK GBR	44.41
3	Davis Kamoga UGA	44.53
4	Alvin Harrison USA	44.62
5	IWAN THOMAS GBR	44.70
6	Roxbert Martin JAM	44.83
7	Davian Clarke JAM	44.99
GB: Du'aine Ladejo 2rh3 6		45.62

800m:

1	Vebjoern Rodal NOR	1:42.58 OR
2	Ezekiel Sepeng RSA	1:42.74

3	Fred Onyancha KEN	1:42.79
4	Norbert Tellez CUB	1:42.85
5	Nico Motchebon GER	1:43.91
6	David Kiptoo KEN	1:44.19
7	Johnny Gray USA	1:44.21
8	Benyounes Lahlou MAR	1:45.52
GB: Craig Winrow SFh1 8		1:48.57
Curtis Robb SFh2		1:47.48
David Strang 1rh6 4		1:47.96

1500m:

1	Noureddine Morceli ALG	3:35.78
2	Fermin Cacho ESP	3:36.40
3	Stephen Kipkorir KEN	3:36.72
4	Laban Rotich KEN	3:37.39
5	William Tanui KEN	3:37.42
6	Abdi Bile SOM	3:38.03
7	Marko Koers NED	3:38.13
8	Ali Hakimi TUN	3:38.19
11	JOHN MAYOCK GBR	3:40.18
12	Hicham El Guerrouj MAR	3:40.75
GB: Anthony Whiteman SFh2 7		3:36.11
Kevin McKay SFh2		3:43.61

5000m:

1	Venuste Niyongabo BUR	13:07.96
2	Paul Bitok KEN	13:08.16
3	Khalid Boulami MAR	13:08.37
4	Dieter Baumann GER	13:08.81
5	Tom Nyariki KEN	13:12.29
6	Bob Kennedy USA	13:12.35
7	Enrique Molina ESP	13:12.91
8	Brahim Lahlafi MAR	13:13.26
GB: John Nuttall SFh2		14:08.39

10,000m:

1	Haile Gebresilasie ETH	27:07.34 OR
2	Paul Tergat KEN	27:08.17

3	Salah Hissou MAR	27:28.59
4	Aloys Nizigama BUR	27:33.79
5	Josephat Machuka KEN	27:35.08
6	Paul Koech KEN	27:35.19
7	Khalid Skah MAR	27:46.98
8	Mathias Ntawulikura RWA	27:50.73
10	JON BROWN GBR	27:59.72

PAUL EVANS GBR dnf

Marathon:

1	Josia Thugwane RSA	2:12:36
2	Bong Ju Lee KOR	2:12:39
3	Erik Wainaina KEN	2:12:44
4	Martin Fiz ESP	2:13:20
5	RICHARD NERURKAR GBR	2:13:39
6	German Silva MEX	2:14:29
7	Steve Moneghetti AUS	2:14:35
8	Benjamin Paredes MEX	2:14:55
55	PETER WHITEHEAD GBR	2:22:37
60	STEVE BRACE GBR	2:23:28

3000m Steeplechase:

1	Joseph Keter KEN	8:07.12
2	Moses Kiptanui KEN	8:08.33
3	Alessandro Lambruschini ITA	8:11.28
4	Matthew Birir KEN	8:17.18
5	Mark Croghan USA	8:17.84
6	Stefan Brand GER	8:18.52
7	Brahim Boulami MAR	8:23.18
8	Jim Svenoy NOR	8:23.39
GB: Keith Cullen SFh1 11		8:46.74
Justin Chaston SFh2 9		8:28.50
Spencer Duval 1rh1 10		8:46.76

110m Hurdles (+0.6):

1	Allen Johnson USA	12.95 OR
2	Mark Crear USA	13.09
3	Florian Schwarthoff GER	13.17

4	COLIN JACKSON GBR	13.19
5	Emilo Valle CUB	13.20
6	Eugene Swift USA	13:23
7	Kyle Vander-Kyup AUS	13.40
8	Erik Batte CUB	13.43
B:	Andy Tulloch r2h4 6	13.68
	ny Jarrett r2h4 dsq	

00m Hurdles:

1	Derrick Adkins USA	47.54
2	Samuel Matete ZAM	47.78
3	Calvin Davis USA	47.96
4	Sven Nylander SWE	47.98
5	Rohan Robinson AUS	48.30
6	Fabrizio Mori ITA	48.41
7	Everson Teixeira BRA	48.57
8	Eronilde de Araujo BRA	48.87
B:	Jon Ridgeon SFh1 7	49.43
	ter Crampton 1rh1 6	49.78
	ary Jennings 1rh7 6	50.41

High Jump:

1	Charles Austin USA	2.39 OR
2	Artur Partyka POL	2.37
3	STEVE SMITH GBR	2.35
4	Dragutin Topic YUG	2.32
5	Steinar Hoen NOR	2.32
6	Lambros Papakostas GRE	2.32
7	Tim Forsyth AUS	2.32
8	Lee Jin-Taek KOR	2.29
B:	Dalton Grant Qual	2.26

Pole Vault:

1	Jean Galfione FRA	5.92 OR
2	Igor Trandenkov RUS	5.92
3	Andrei Tivontchik GER	5.92
4	Igor Potapovich KZK	5.86
5	Pyotr Bochkaryov RUS	5.86
6	Dmitriy Markov BLR	5.86
7	Tim Lobinger GER	5.80
8	Lawrence Johnson USA	5.70
B:	Nick Buckfield Qual	5.40

Long Jump:

1	Carl Lewis USA	8.50
2	James Beckford JAM	8.29

3	Joe Greene USA	8.24
4	Emmanuel Bangue FRA	8.19
5	Mike Powell USA	8.17
6	Gregor Cankar SLO	8.11
7	Aleksandr Glovatskiy BLR	8.07
8	Mattis Sunneborn SWE	8.06

Triple Jump:

1	Kenny Harrison USA	18.09 OR
2	JONATHAN EDWARDS GBR	17.88
3	Yoelbi Quesada CUB	17.44
4	Mike Conley USA	17.40
5	Armen Martirosyan ARM	16.97
6	Brian Wellman BER	16.95
7	Galin Georgiev BUL	16.92
8	Robert Howard USA	16.90
GB:	Francis Agyepong Qual	16.71

Shot Put:

1	Randy Barnes USA	21.62
2	John Godina USA	20.79
3	Oleksandr Bagach UKR	20.75
4	Paolo Dal Sogilo ITA	20.74
5	Oliver-Sven Buder GER	20.51
6	Roman Virastyuk UKR	20.45
7	C J Hunter USA	20.39
8	Dragan Peric YUG	20.07
GB:	Shaun Pickering Qual	18.29

Discus:

1	Lars Riedel GER	69.40 OR
2	Vladimir Dubrovshchik BLR	66.60
3	Vasiliy Kaptyukh BLR	65.80
4	Anthony Washington USA	65.42
5	Virgilijus Alekna LIT	65.30
6	Jurgen Schult GER	64.42
7	Vitaliy Sidorov UKR	63.78
8	Vaclovas Kidykas LIT	62.78
GB:	Robert Weir Qual	
	Glen Smith Qual	

Hammer:

1	Balazs Kiss HUN	81.24
2	Lance Deal HUN	81.12
3	Olksiy Krykun UKR	80.02
4	Andriy Skvaruk UKR	79.92

5	Heinz Weis GER	79.78
6	Ilya Konovalov RUS	78.82
7	Igor Astapkovich BLR	78.20
8	Sergey Alay BLR	77.38
GB:	David Smith Qual	69.32

Javelin:

1	Jan Zelezny CZE	88.16
2	STEVE BACKLEY GBR	87.44
3	Seppo Raty FIN	86.98
4	Raymond Hecht GER	86.88
5	Boris Henry GER	85.68
6	Sergey Makarov RUS	85.30
7	Kimmo Kinnunen FIN	84.02
8	Tom Pukstys USA	83.58
GB:	Mick Hill Qual	80.48
	Nick Nieland Qual	75.74

Decathlon:

1	Dan O'Brien USA	8824
2	Frank Busemann GER	8706
3	Tomas Dvorak CZE	8664
4	Steve Fritz USA	8644
5	Edurd Hamalainen BLR	8613
6	Erki Nool EST	8543
7	Robert Zmelik CZE	8422
8	Ramil Ganiyev UZB	8318
	ALEX KRUGER GBR dnf	

20km Walk:

1	Jefferson Perez ECU	1:20:07
2	Ilya Markov RUS	1:20:16
3	Bernardo Segura MEX	1:20:03
4	Nick A'Hern AUS	1:20:31
5	Rishat Shafikov RUS	1:20:41
6	Aigars Fadejevs LAT	1:20:47
7	Mikhail Shchennikov RUS	1:21:09
8	Robert Korzeniowski POL	1:21:13

50km Walk:

1	Robert Korzeniowski POL	3:43:30
2	Mikhail Shchennikov RUS	3:43:46
3	Valentin Massana ESP	3:44:19
4	Arturo di Mezza ITA	3:44:52
5	Viktor Ginko BLR	3:45:27
6	Ignacio Zamudio MEX	3:46:07

7	Valentin Kononen FIN	3:47:40
8	Sergey Korepanov KZK	3:48:42
34	CHRIS MADDOCKS GBR	4:18:41

4x100m:

1	Canada	37.69
2	USA	38.05
3	Brazil	38.41
4	Ukraine	38.55
5	Sweden	38.67
6	Cuba	39.39
	France dnf	
	Ghana dns	
	GBR 1rh3 dnf	

4x400m:

| 1 | USA | 2:55.99 |
| 2 | GREAT BRITAIN | |

(Iwan Thomas, Jamie Baulch, Mark Richardson, Roger Black; Du'aine Ladejo ran heat & semi, Mark Hylton ran heat) 2:56.60 ER

3	Jamaica	2:59.42
4	Senegal	3:00.64
5	Japan	3:00.76
6	Poland	3:00.96
7	Bahamas	3:02.71
	Kenya dns	

WOMEN

100m (-0.7):

1	Gail Devers USA	10.94
2	Merlene Ottey JAM	10.94
3	Gwen Torrence USA	10.96
4	Chandra Sturrup BAH	11.00
5	Marina Trandenkova RUS	11.06
6	Natalya Voronova RUS	11.10
7	Mary Onyali NGR	11.13
8	Zhanna Pintusevych UKR	11.14
GB:	Stephanie Douglas 2rh1 8	11.75
	Marcia Richardson 2rh2 7	11.55
	Simmone Jacobs 2rh3 5	11.47

200m (+0.3):

1	Marie-Jose Perec FRA	22.12
2	Merlene Ottey JAM	22.24
3	Mary Onyali NGR	22.38
4	Inger Miller USA	22.41
5	Galina Malchugina RUS	22.45
6	Chandra Sturrup BAH	22.54
7	Juliet Cuthbert JAM	22.60
8	Carlette Guidry USA	22.61
GB:	Katharine Merry 2rh2 5	23.17
	Simmone Jacobs 2rh3 6	22.96

400m:

1	Marie-Jose Perec FRA	48.25 OR
2	Cathy Freeman AUS	48.63
3	Falilat Ogunkoya NGR	49.10
4	Pauline Davis BAH	49.28
5	Jearl Miles USA	49.55
6	Fatima Yusuf NGR	49.77
7	Sandie Richards JAM	50.45
8	Grit Breuer GER	50.71
GB:	Donna Fraser 2rh1 7	51.58
	Phylis Smith 2rh4 6	52.16

800m:

1	Svetlana Masterkova RUS	1:57.73
2	Ana Quirot CUB	1:58.11
3	Maria Mutola MOZ	1:58.71
4	KELLY HOLMES GBR	1:58.81
5	Yelena Afanasyeva RUS	1:59.57
6	Patricia Djate FRA	1:59.61
7	Natalya Dukhnova BLR	2:00.32
8	Toni Hodgkinson NZL	2:00.54
GB:	Diane Modahl 1rh1 dnf	

1500m:

1	Svetlana Masterkova RUS	4:00.83
2	Gabriela Szabo ROM	4:01.54
3	Theresia Kiesl AUT	4:03.02
4	Leah Pells CAN	4:03.56
5	Margaret Crowley AUS	4:03.79
6	Carla Sacramento POR	4:03.91
7	Lyudmila Borisova RUS	4:05.90
8	Malgorzata Rydz POL	4:05.92
11	KELLY HOLMES GBR	4:07.46

5000m:

1	Wang Junxia CHN	14:59.88 OR
2	Pauline Konga KEN	15:03.49
3	Roberta Brunet ITA	15:07.52
4	Michiko Shimizu JPN	15:09.05
5	PAULA RADCLIFFE GBR	15:13.11
6	Yelena Romanova RUS	15:14.09
7	Elena Fidatov ROM	15:16.71
8	Rose Cheruiyot KEN	15:17.33
GB:	Alison Wyeth 1rh1 15	16:24.74
	Sonia McGeorge 1rh3 13	16:01.92

10,000m:

1	Fernanda Riberio POR	31:01.63 OR
2	Wang Junxia CHN	31:02.58
3	Gete Wami ETH	31:06.65
4	Derartu Tulu ETH	31:10.46
5	Masako Chiba JPN	31:20.62
6	Tegla Loroupe KEN	31:23.22
7	Yuko Kawakami JPN	31:23.23
8	Iulia Negura ROM	31:26.64

Marathon:

1	Fatuma Roba ETH	2:26:05
2	Valentina Yegorova RUS	2:28:05
3	Yuko Arimori JPN	2:28:39
4	Katrin Dorre-Heinig GER	2:28:45
5	Rocio Rios ESP	2:30:05
6	Lidia Simon ROM	2:31:04
7	Manuela Machado POR	2:31:11
8	Sonja Krolik GER	2:31:16
16	LIZ McCOLGAN GBR	2:34:30
45	KAREN MACLEOD GBR	2:42:08
58	SUZANNE RIGG GBR	2:52:09

00m Hurdles (+0.2):

1	Ludmila Engquist SWE	12.58
2	Brigita Bukovec SLO	12.59
3	Patricia Girard-Leno FRA	12.65
4	Gail Devers USA	12.66
5	Dionne Rose JAM	12.74
6	Michelle Freeman JAM	12.76
7	Lynda Goode USA	13.11

atalya Shekhodanova RUS dsq

B: Angela Thorp SFh1 5   12.80 UKR

KR Jacqui Agyepong 1rh1 7   13.24

00m Hurdles:

1	Deon Hemmings JAM	52.82 OR
2	Kim Batten USA	53.08
3	Tonja Buford-Bailey USA	53.22
4	Debbie Paris JAM	53.97
5	Heike Meissner GER	54.03
6	Rosey Edeh CAN	54.39
7	Ionela Tirlea ROM	54.40
8	Silvia Rieger GER	54.57

B: Sally Gunnell SFh2 dnf 1rh2 2   55.29

High Jump:

1	Stefka Kostadinova BUL	2.05 OR
2	Niki Bakogianni GRE	2.03
3	Inga Babakova UKR	2.01
4	Yelena Gulyayeva RUS	1.99
5 =	Alina Astafei GER	1.96
5 =	Tatyana Motkova RUS	1.96
5 =	Nele Zilinskiene LIT	1.96

ntonella Bevilacqua ITA dsq

B: Debbie Marti Qual   1.85

ea Haggett Qual   1.90

Long Jump:

1	Chioma Ajunwa NGR	7.12
2	Fiona May ITA	7.02
3	Jackie Joyner-Kersee USA	7.00
4	Niki Xanthou GRE	6.97
5	Iryna Chekhovtsova UKR	6.97
6	Agata Karczmarek POL	6.90
7	Nicole Boegman AUS	6.73
8	Tunde Vaszi HUN	6.60

va Prandzheva BUL dsq

B: Denise Lewis Qual   6.33

Triple Jump:

1	Inessa Kravets UKR	15.33 OR
2	Inna Lasovskaya RUS	14.98
3	Sarka Kasparkova CZE	14.98
4	ASHIA HANSEN GBR	14.49
5	Olga Vasdeki GRE	14.44
6	Ren Ruipeng CHN	14.30
7	Rodica Mateescu ROM	14.21
8	Jelena Blazevica LAT	14.12

Iva Prandzheva BUL dsq

GB: Michelle Griffith Qual   13.70

Shot Put:

1	Astrid Kumbernuss GER	20.56
2	Sui Xinmei CHN	19.88
3	Irina Khudorozhkina RUS	19.35
4	Vita Pavlysh UKR	19.30
5	Connie Price-Smith USA	19.22
6	Stephanie Storp GER	19.06
7	Kathrin Neimke GER	18.92
8	Irina Korzhaenko RUS	18.65

GB: Judy Oakes Qual   18.56

Discus:

1	Ilke Wyludda GER	69.66
2	Natalya Sadova RUS	66.48
3	Elya Zvereva BLR	65.64
4	Franka Dietzsch GER	65.48
5	Xiao Yanling CHN	64.72
6	Olga Chernyavskaya RUS	64.70
7	Nicoleta Grasu ROM	63.28
8	Lisa-Marie Vizaniari AUS	62.48

GB: Jacqui McKernan Qual   58.88

Javelin:

1	Heli Rantanen FIN	67.94
2	Louise McPaul AUS	65.54
3	Trine Hattestad NOR	64.98
4	Isel Lopez CUB	64.68
5	Xiomara Rivero CUB	64.48
6	Karen Forkel GER	64.18
7	Mikaela Ingberg FIN	61.52
8	Li Lei CHN	60.74

GB: Tessa Sanderson Qual   58.86

Shelley Holroyd   54.72

Hepathlon:

1	Ghada Shouaa SYR	6780
2	Natasha Sazanovich BLR	6563
3	DENISE LEWIS GBR	6489
4	Urszula Wlodarczyk POL	6484
5	Eunice Barber SLE	6342
6	Rita Inancsi HUN	6336
7	Sabine Braun GER	6317
8	Kelly Blair USA	6307

10km Walk:

1	Yelena Nikolayeva RUS	41:49 OR
2	Elisabetta Perrone ITA	42:12
3	Wang Yan CHN	42:19
4	Gu Yan CHN	42:34
5	Rossela Giordano ITA	42:43
6	Olya Kardapoltseva BLR	43:02
7	Katarzyna Radtke POL	43:05
8	Valya Tsybulskaya BLR	43:21

33 VICKY LUPTON GBR   47:05

4x100m:

1	USA	41.95
2	Bahamas	42.14
3	Jamaica	42.24
4	Russia	42.27
5	Nigeria	42.56
6	France	42.76
7	Australia	43.70
8	GREAT BRITAIN (Angela Thorp, Marcia Richardson, Simmone Jacobs, Katharine Merry)	43.93

4x400m:

1	USA	3:20.91
2	Nigeria	3:21.04
3	Germany	3:21.14
4	Jamaica	3:21.69
5	Russia	3:22.22
6	Cuba	3:25.85
7	Czech Republic	3:26.99
8	France	3:28.46

GBR 1rh1 4   3:28.13

GBR v Russia Indoor International
Birmingham, 27 January

MEN:

60m:	Gardener GBR	6.55
200m:	Wariso GBR	21.03
400m:	Hylton GBR	46.96
800m:	Loginov RUS	1:50.54
1500m:	Whiteman GBR	3:39.47
3000m:	Kashayev RUS	7:58.79
60mh:	Vetrov RUS	7.85
HJ:	Grant GBR	2.34m
PV:	Smyiryagin RUS	5.55m
LJ:	Sosunov RUS	8.06m
TJ:	Kurennoi RUS	16.49m
SP:	Pickering GBR	19.10m
4x400m	GBR	3:08.47
Teams:	GBR 69, RUS 68	

WOMEN:

60m:	Anisimova RUS	7.37
200m	Goncharenko RUS	23.28
400m:	Andreyeva RUS	53.49
800m:	Korzh RUS	2:05.32
1500m:	Biriukova RUS	4:13.05
3000m:	McGeorge GBR	9:28.04
60mh	Court GBR	8.35
HJ:	Golodnova RUS	1.95m
PV:	Abramova RUS	4.00m
LJ:	D Lewis GBR	6.45m
TJ:	Kayukova RUS	13.90m
SP:	Oakes GBR	18.63m
4x400m:	RUS	3:31.88
Teams:	RUS 80, GBR 67	

AAA Indoor Championships
Birmingham, 3–4 February

MEN:

60m:	Michael Rosswess	6.68
200m:	Doug Turner	21.06
400m:	Mark Hylton	46.45
800m:	Martin Steele	1:51.21
1500m:	Terry West	3:49.90
3000m:	Matt Skelton	8:00.48
60mh:	Neil Owen	7.81
HJ:	Michael Robbins	2.19m
PV:	Nick Buckfield	5.61m
LJ:	Chris Davidson	7.34m

TJ:	Francis Agyepong	16.55m
SP:	Shaun Pickering	17.88m
Hept:	Stephen Rogers	5252

WOMEN:

60m:	Marcia Richardson	7.34
200m:	Catherine Murphy	23.69
400m:	Melanie Neef	52.50
800m:	Vicky Sterne	2:06.41
1500m:	Angela Davies	4:16.24
60mh:	Jacqui Agyepong	8.17
HJ:	Michelle Dunkley	1.85m
PV:	Kate Staples	3.70m
LJ:	Ann Brooks	6.01m
TJ:	Michelle Griffith	13.18m
SP:	Judy Oakes	18.57m
Pent:	Sarah Damm	4058

Interflora Classic IAAF Indoor Grand Prix
Birmingham, 10 February

MEN:

60m:	D Ezinwa NGR	6.58
200m:	Moen NOR	20.69
400m:	D Hall USA	45.99
1000m:	Malakwen KEN	2:19.11
3000m:	Kiptanui KEN	7:38.60
60mh:	Jarrett GBR	7.62
HJ:	S Smith GBR	2.36m
PV:	Starkey USA	5.60m

WOMEN:

60m:	Opara NGR	7.20
400m:	Hemmings JAM	53.16
1000m:	Mutola MOZ	2:32.08 WIR
60mh:	Russell JAM	8.03
HJ:	Marti GBR	1.89m
PV:	Muller GER	3.90m
TJ:	Hansen GBR	14.58m

GBR v France Indoor International
Glasgow, 24 February

MEN:

60m:	John GBR	6.62
200m:	Regis GBR	20.88
400m:	Ladejo GBR	46.39
800m:	Vialettes FRA	1:50.35
1500m:	Chekhemani FRA	3:46.35

3000m:	Dubus FRA	7:58.47
60mh:	Philibert FRA	7.71
HJ:	Grant GBR	2.26m
PV:	Andji FRA	5.60m
LJ:	Ducros FRA	7.69m
TJ:	Agyepong GBR	16.29m
SP:	Proctor GBR	18.09m
4x400m:	GBR	3:07.72
Teams:	GBR 72, FRA 66	

WOMEN:

60m:	Kinch GBR	7.33
200m:	Dia FRA	23.77
400m:	Gunnell GBR	53.28
800m:	Djate FRA	2:03.33
1500m:	Gunning GBR	4:17.02
3000m:	Duquenoy FRA	9:05.44
60mh:	Tourrett FRA	8.09
HJ:	Marti GBR	1.89m
PV:	Staples GBR	3.85m
LJ:	D Lewis GBR	6.48m
TJ:	Griffith GBR	13.51m
SP:	Oakes GBR	18.59m
4x400m:	FRA	3:36.25
Teams:	FRA 70, GBR 69	

European Indoor Championships
Stockholm, 8–10 March

MEN:

60m:	1, Marc Blume GER	6.62
	2, JASON JOHN GBR	6.64
	3, Peter Karlsson SWE	6.64
	6, KEVIN WILLIAMS GBR	6.72
200m:	1, Erik Wijmeersch BEL	21.04
	2, Alexios Alexopoulos GRE	21.05
	3, Toprbjorn Eriksson SWE	21.07
400m:	1, DU'AINE LADEJO GBR	46.12
	2, Pierre-Maria Hilaire FRA	46.82
	3, Ashraf Saber ITA	46.86
800m:	1, Roberto Parra ESP	1:47.74
	2, Giuseppe D'Urso ITA	1:48.04
	3, Wojchiech Kaldowski POL	1:48.40
1500m:	1, Mateo Canellas ESP	3:44.50
	2, TONY WHITEMAN GBR	3:44.78
	3, Abdelkader Chekhemani FRA	3:45.96
3000m:	1, Anacleto Jimenez ESP	7:50.06
	2, Christoph Impens BEL	7:50.19
	3, Panayiotis Papoulias GRE	7:50.80
60mh:	1, Igor Kazanov LAT	7.59
	2, Guntins Peders LAT	7.65
	3, Jonathan N'Senga BEL	7.66
HJ:	1, Dragutin Topic YUG	2.35
	2, Leonid Pumalainen RUS	2.33
	3, Steinar Hoen NOR	2.31
PV:	1, Dmitri Markov BLR	5.85
	2, Viktor Chistyakov RUS	5.80
	3, Pyotr Bockhkaryov RUS	5.80
	7, NICK BUCKFIELD GBR	5.55

LJ:	1, Mattias Sunneborn SWE	8.06
	2, Bogdan Tarus ROM	8.03
	3, Spyridon Vasadekis GRE	8.03
TJ:	1, Maris Bruziks LAT	16.97
	2, FRANCIS AGYEPONG GBR	16.93
	3, Armen Mrtirosyan ARM	16.74
SP:	1, Paolo Dal Soglio ITA	20.50
	2, Dirk Urban GER	20.04
	3, Oliver-Sven Buder GER	19.91
Hept:	1, Erik Nool EST	6188
	2, Tomas Dvorak CZE	6114
	3, Jon Armar Magnusson ISR	6069

WOMEN:

60m:	1, Ekaterini Thanou GER	7.15
	2, Odiah Sidibe FRA	7.25
	3, Jerneja Perec SLO	7.28
200m:	1, Sandra Myers ESP	23.15
	2, Erika Suchovska CZE	23.16
	3, Zlakta Georgieva BUL	23.40
400m:	1, Grit Breuer GER	50.81
	2, Olga Kotlyarova RUS	51.70
	3, Tatyana Chebykina RUS	51.71
800m:	1, Patricia Djate FRA	2:01.71
	2, Stella Jongmans NED	2:01.88
	3, Svetlana Masterkova RUS	2:02.86
1500m:	1, Carla Sacramento POR	4:08.95
	2, Yekaterina Podkopayeva RUS	4:09.65
	3, Malgorzata Rydz POL	4:10.50
3000m:	1, Fernanda Riberio POR	8:39.49
	2, Sara Wedlund SWE	8:50.32
	3, Marta Dominguez ESP	8:53.34
60mh:	1, Patricia Girard FRA	7.89
	2, Brigita Bukovec SLO	7.90
	3, Monique Tourret FRA	8.09
HJ:	1, Alina Astafei GER	1.98
	2, Niko Bakogianni GRE	1.96
	3, Olga Bolshova MOL	1.94
PV:	1, Vala Flosadottir ISL	4.16
	2, Christine Adams GER	4.05
	3, Bagriela Mihalcea ROM	4.50
LJ:	1, Renata Nielsen DEN	6.76
	2, Yelena Sinehukova RUS	6.75
	3, Claudia Gerhardt GER	6.74
TJ:	1, Iva Prandzeva BUL	14.54
	2, Sarka Kasparkova CZE	14.50
	3, Olga Vasdeki GRE	14.30
SP:	1, Astrid Kumbernuss GER	19.79
	2, Irina Khudorzhkina RUS	19.07
	3, Valentina Fedyushina UKR	18.90
	4, JUDY OAKES GBR	18.72
Pent:	1, Yelena Lebedyenko RUS	4685
	2, Urszula Wolddarczyk POL	4597
	3, Irina Vostrikova RUS	4545

European Cup Super League
Madrid, 1–2 June

MEN:

100m (+0.8):	1, Christie GBR	10.04
200m (+2.5):	1, Christie GBR	20.25
400m:	1, Jahn GER	45.64
	2, Ladejo GBR	45.72
800m:	1, Parra ESP	1:44.97
	4, Strang GBR	1:46.38
1500m:	1, Cacho ESP	3:40.24
	3, Whiteman GBR	3:41.21
3000m:	1, Baumann GER	7:57.19
	8, Lough GBR	8:11.44
5000m:	1, Di Napoli ITA	13:52.34
	4, Cullen GBR	14:00.61
3000ms/c:	1, Brand GER	8:30.09
	3, Chaston GBR	8:33.59
110mh (-0.3):	1, Schwarthoff GER	13.20
	2, Jackson GBR	13.63
400mh:	1, Mori ITA	49.45
	2, Ridgeon GBR	49.84
HJ:	1, Ortiz ESP	2.27
	3, Grant GBR	2.27
PV:	1, Bochkariov RUS	5.70
	4, Buckfield GBR	5.50
LJ:	1, Bianchi ITA	8.25
	9, Salle GBR	7.43
TJ:	1, Edwards GBR	17.79
SP:	1, Dal Soglio ITA	20.72
	6, Pickering GBR	19.23
DT:	1, Martinez ESP	62.38
	5, Weir GBR	61.02
HT:	1, Kobs GER	78.18
	8, M Jones GBR	71.74
JT:	1, Hecht GER	88.86
	5, Mackenzie GBR	74.10
4x100m:	1, Ukraine	38.53
	3, GBR	38.67
4x400m:	1, GBR	3:03.38

Final Positions:

	1, Germany	142
	2, Great Britain	125
	3, Italy	110
	4, Spain	106
	5, Russia	103
	6, France	93.5
	7, Ukraine	84
	8, Sweden	75.5
	9, Finland	53

WOMEN:

100m (+0.3):	1, Trandenkov RUS	11.14
	7, Jacobs GBR	11.51
200m (+1.6):	1, Perec FRA	22.34
	3, Merry GBR	22.88
400m:	1, Breuer GER	50.22
	7, Fraser GBR	52.37
800m:	1, Masterkova RUS	1:57.87
	2, Holmes GBR	1:58.20
1500m:	1, Churbanova RUS	4:09.57
	7, Davies GBR	4:14.56;
3000m:	1, Bitzner FRA	8:59.82
	5, McGeorge GBR	9:09.53
5000m:	1, Wessel GER	15:40.36
	7, Whitcombe GBR	16:41.46
100mh (+0.7):	1, Bodrova UKR	12.89
	3, Thorp GBR	13.09
400mh:	1, Gunnell GBR	56.84
HJ:	1, Astafei GER	1.98
	7, Haggett GBR	1.84
LJ:	1, Prandzheva BUL	6.84
	4, Lewis GBR	6.66
TJ:	1, Hansen GBR	14.57
SP:	1, Kumbernuss GER	20.05
	2, Oakes GBR	19.00
DT:	1, Wyludda GER	65.66
	8, Callaway GBR	50.86
JT:	1, Ovchinnikova RUS	65.72
	4, Sanderson GBR	58.18
4x100m:	1, Russia	42.55
	7, GBR	44.07
4x400m:	1, Germany	3:26.19
	5, GBR	3:31.80

Final Positions:

	1, Germany	115
	2, Russia	97
	3, Belarus	79
	4, Ukraine	78
	5, France	75
	6, Great Britain	73
	7, Spain	49
	8, Bulgaria	46

Securicor AAA Championships
Birmingham, 14–16 June

MEN:

100m (+0.1):	Linford Christie	10.04
200m (-0.5):	John Regis	20.54
400m:	Roger Black	44.39 UKR
800m:	Curtis Robb	1:47.61
1500m:	John Mayock	3:37.03
5000m:	John Nuttall	13:48.35
10,000m:	Rob Denmark	28:20.80
3000ms/c:	Justin Chaston	8:29.19
110mh (-0.1):	Colin Jackson	13.13
400mh:	Jon Ridgeon	49.16
HJ:	Steve Smith	2.31m
PV:	Nick Buckfield	5.71m UKR
LJ:	Darren Ritchie	7.86m
TJ:	Francis Agyepong	17.12m
SP:	Matt Simson	18.82m
DT:	Robert Weir	60.02m
HT:	David Smith	72.58m

| JT: Nick Nieland | 83.06m |
| 10kW: Steve Partington | 42:29.73 |

WOMEN:

100m (-1.1): Stephanie Douglas	11.55
200m: Simmone Jacobs	23.11
400m: Phylis Smith	51.74
800m: Kelly Holmes	1:57.84
1500m: Kelly Holmes	4:08.14
5000m: Paula Radcliffe	15:28.46
10,000m: Louise Watson	33:21.46
100mh(-2.3): Angela Thorp	13.26
400mh: Sally Gunnell	54.65
HJ: Debbie Marti	1.94m
PV: Kate Staples	3.80m
LJ: Denise Lewis	6.55m
TJ: Ashia Hansen	14.25m
SP: Judy Oakes	18.65m
DT: Jackie McKernan	54.12
HT: Lyn Sprules	54.16m
JT: Tessa Sanderson	62.88m
5kW: Vicky Lupton	23:04.57

BUPA Games
Gateshead, 30 June

MEN:

100m(+2.4): Christie GBR	10.16
200m(+2.9):Whitted USA	20.53
400m: Thomas GBR	44.94
800m: Sepeng RSA	1:46.00
1500m: Kennedy USA	3:40.97
5000m: Evans GBR	13:47.70
110mh(+2.9): Jackson GBR	13.24
400mh: Thomas GBR	48.85
HJ: Smith GBR	2.28m
PV: Manson USA & Miller AUS	5.60m
TJ: Edwards GBR	17.02m
SP: Buder GER	20.09m
JT: Pukstys USA	84.04m

WOMEN:

100m(+1.5): Richardson GBR	11.44
200m (+3.1): Guidry USA	22.55
400m: Freeman AUS	49.96
800m: Holmes GBR	1:59.82
1500m: Crowley AUS	4:14.43
100mh(+2.3): Thorp GBR	12.95
TJ: Hansen GBR	14.14m
DT: Wyludda GER	65.20m

BUPA Challenge, GBR v International Select
Gateshead, 19 August

MEN:

100m (-0.3): Bailey IS	10.19
200m (-1.6): Regis GBR	20.62
400m: Black GBR	44.64
1500m: Mayock GBR	3:37.75
3000m: Caddy GBR	8:03.59
110mh(+0.5): Johnson IS	13.25
400mh: Davis IS	48.99
HJ: Austin IS	2.30m
PV: Manson IS	5.60m
TJ: Edwards GBR	17.38
JT: Pykstys IS	85.38
4x400m: GBR	2:59.85

WOMEN:

200m (-1.0): Cuthbert IS	23.04
400m: Graham IS	51.24
800m: Turner IS	2:06.54
1500m: Pells IS	4:09.24
100mh(-0.4): Rose IS	12.99
HJ: Marti GBR	1.90m
TJ: Hansen GBR	14.51m
JT: Rivero IS	63.64m
Teams: GBR 121, IS 121	
GRY 121	

McDonald's Games
Sheffield, 25 August

MEN:

100m (+0.9): O Ezinwa NGR	10.06
200m (+1.9): Williams USA	20.45
400m: Black GBR	45.05
800m: Rodal NOR	1:44.93
Emsley	
Carr Mile: Tanui KEN	3:54.57
110mh (+1.8): Johnson USA	13.07
400mh: Robinson AUS	49.39
HJ: Austin USA	2.30m
PV: Barthel NOR	5.60m
TJ: Edwards GBR	16.90m
HT: Head GBR	72.44m
JT: Pukstys USA	86.62m

WOMEN:

100m(+0.9): Smith GBR	11.49
200m (+3.1): Freeman AUS	22.90
400m: Malone USA	51.50
800m: Crooks CAN	2:00.42
3000m: Cheruiyot KEN	9:02.68
100mh(+1.6): Rose JAM	12.83
400mh: Hemmings JAM	55.13
HJ: Marti GBR	1.90m
TJ: Kasparkova CZE	14.84m
JT: Lopez CUB	61.36m

Rio Grand Prix

Rio de Janeiro, 4 May

MEN:

100m (+0.6):	Donovan Bailey CAN	10.07
400m:	Derek Mills USA	45.23
1500m:	Venuste Niyongabo BUR	3:37.03
3000m:	Shem Kororia KEN	7:51.13
400mh:	Danny Harris USA	48.08
HJ:	Javier Sotomayor CUB	2.28m
PV:	Sergey Bubka UKR	5.75m

WOMEN:

100m (-1.8):	Gwen Torrence USA	11.13
400m:	Falilat Ogunkoya NGR	50.69
100mh (0.0):	Aliuska Lopez CUB	13.15
LJ:	Fiona May ITA	6.86m
JT:	Jette Jeppesen DEN	64.66m

Osaka Grand Prix

Osaka, 11 May

MEN:

100m (-0.8):	Frankie Fredericks NAM	10.09
Mile:	Noureddine Morceli ALG	3:51.30
5000m:	Julius Gitahi KEN	13:29.28
400mh:	Samuel Matete ZAM	48.15
HJ:	Lee Jin-taek KOR	2.30m
TJ:	Zou Sixin CHN	16.95m
SP:	John Godina USA	20.85m
HT:	Igor Astapkovich BLR	79.36m

WOMEN:

100m (-2.2):	Chryste Gaines USA	11.36
5000m:	Catherina McKiernan IRL	15:07.36
100mh (+0.4):	Michelle Freeman JAM	12.79
JT:	Mikaela Ingberg FIN	65.66m

Atlanta Grand Prix

Atlanta, 18 May

MEN:

100m (+2.1):	Dennis Mitchell USA	9.93
400m:	Butch Reynolds USA	44.33
Mile:	Noureddine Morceli ALG	3:50.86
3000m:	Paul Bitok KEN	7:47.80
400mh:	Bryan Bronson USA	48.66
HJ:	Javier Sotomayor CUB	2.33m

PV:	Sergey Bubka UKR	6.02m
TJ:	Jonathan Edwards GBR	17.59m
SP:	John Godina USA	21.11m
HT:	Igor Astapkovich BLR	78.68m

WOMEN:

100m (+1.6):	Gwen Torrence USA	10.85
400m:	Marie-Jose Perec FRA	50.17
1500m:	Julie Henner USA	4:15.24
100mh (+2.9):	Dionne Rose JAM	12.76
LJ:	Jackie Joyner-Kersee USA	7.20m
DT:	Lisa-Marie Vizaniare AUS	64.54m

Prefontaine Classic

Eugene, 26 May

MEN:

100m (+1.8):	Olapade Adeniken NGR	10.13
400m:	Calvin Harrison USA	44.72
Mile:	David Kibet KEN	3:52.28
400mh:	Danny Harris USA	48.90
HJ:	Charles Austin USA	2.34m
PV:	Sergey Bubka UKR	5.70m
TJ:	Jerome Romain DMN	16.93m
SP:	John Godina USA	20.55m
HT:	Balazs Kiss HUN	79.86m

WOMEN:

100m (+1.8):	Gwen Torrence USA	10.96
400m:	Cathy Freeman AUS	50.40
1500m:	Maria Mutola MOZ	4:06.86
3000m:	Sonia O'Sullivan IRL	8:39.33
100mh (+2.3):	Cheryl Dickey USA	12.85
LJ:	Shana Williams USA	6.83m
DT:	Lisa-Marie Vizaniare AUS	64.90m

Golden Gala

Rome, 5 June

MEN:

100m (+0.4):	Dennis Mitchell USA	10.05
400m:	Darnell Hall USA	45.13
1500m:	Noureddine Morceli ALG	3:30.93
5000m:	Salah Hissou MAR	12:50.80
400mh:	Samuel Matete ZAM	48.16
HJ:	Dragutin Topic YUG	2.35m
TJ:	Jonathan Edwards GBR	17.55m
SP:	Oliver Buder GER	20.30m
HT:	Igor Astapkovich BLR	79.96m

WOMEN:

100m (+0.3):	Merlene Ottey JAM	11.00
400m:	Falilat Ogunkoya NGR	50.52
1500m:	Kelly Holmes GBR	4:04.56
5000m:	Sonia O'Sullivan IRL	14:54.75
100mh:	Lyudmila Engqvist SWE	12.62
LJ:	Inessa Kravets UKR	6.97m
JT:	Felicia Tilea ROM	66.34m

Znamenskiy Memorial
Moscow, 7 June

MEN:

100m (+0.4):	Olapade Adeniken NGR	10.03
1500m:	Noureddine Morceli ALG	3:33.22
400mh:	Samuel Matete ZAM	48.60
PV:	Sergey Bubka UKR	5.90m
HT:	Igor Astapkovich BLR	79.30

WOMEN:

400m:	Juliet Cuthbert JAM	50.94
1500m:	Olga Churbanova RUS	4:06.32
3000m:	Sonia O'Sullivan IRL	8:47.32
100mh (+0.9):	Gillian Russell JAM	12.87
LJ:	Inessa Kravets UKR	6.99m

Meeting BNP de Paris
Paris, 28 June

MEN:

100m (+0.7):	Bruny Surin CAN	10.03
1500m:	Noureddine Morceli ALG	3:29.50
5000m:	Salah Hissou MAR	12:55.93
400mh:	Derrick Adkins USA	47.70
HJ:	Lee Jin-Taek KOR	2.32m
PV:	Sergey Bubka UKR	6.00m

WOMEN:

100m (-0.1):	Mary Onyali NGR	11.06
400m:	Marie-Jose Perec FRA	49.47
1500m:	Gabriela Szabo ROM	4:03.18
100mh (-0.6):	Patricia Girard FRA	12.86
JT:	Oksana Ovchinnikova RUS	64.60m

Athletissima '96
Lausanne, 3 July

MEN:

100m:	Frankie Fredericks NAM	9.86
200m:	Ato Boldon TRI	19.85
400m:	Michael Johnson USA	43.66
1500m:	Noureddine Morceli ALG	3:30.99
3000m:	Daniel Komen KEN	7:31.33
3000ms/c:	Joseph Keter KEN	8:14.17

110mh:	Allen Johnson USA	13.08
400mh:	Samuel Matate ZAM	47.85
HJ:	Steinar Hoen NOR	2.31m
PV:	Igor Potapovich KZK	5.85m
TJ:	Brian Wellman BER	16.55m
HT:	Balazs Kiss HUN	80.02m

WOMEN:

100m:	Gwen Torrence USA	10.97
400m:	Marie-Jose Perec FRA	49.45
800m:	Maria Mutola MOZ	1:58.16
1500m:	Anita Weyermann SUI	4:03.45
100mh:	Lyudmila Engqvist SWE	12.71
400mh:	Tonja Buford USA	53.61
TJ:	Inessa Kravets UKR	14.76m
JT:	Steffi Nerius GER	66.70m

Bislett Games
Oslo, 5 July

MEN:

100m:	Dennis Mitchell USA	10.10
200m:	Frankie Fredericks NAM	19.82
800m:	Wilson Kipketer DEN	1:42.76
Mile:	Noureddine Morceli ALG	3:48.15
3000m:	Paul Bitok KEN	7:29.55
400mh:	Derrick Adkins USA	48.18
HJ:	Patrik Sjoberg SWE	2.31m
TJ:	Jonathan Edwards GBR	17.68m
DT:	Lars Riedel GER	69.12m
JT:	Gavin Lovegrove NZL	88.20m

WOMEN:

100m:	Merlene Ottey JAM	10.95
400m:	Cathy Freeman AUS	49.81
1500m:	Sonia O'Sullivan IRL	3:59.91
5000m:	Fernanda Riberio POR	14:41.07
100mh:	Lyudmila Engqvist SWE	12.48
HJ:	Stefka Kostadinova BUL	1.98m
DT:	Ilke Wyludda GER	66.66m
JT:	Trine Hattestad NOR	67.06m

DN Galan
Stockholm, 8 July

MEN:

100m (+0.3):	Ato Boldon TRI	10.07
400m:	Anthuan Maybank USA	44.67
1500m:	Hicham El Guerrouj MAR	3:29.59
5000m:	Daniel Komen KEN	12:51.60
400mh:	Torrance Zellner USA	48.91
HJ:	Tim Forsyth AUS	2.30m
TJ:	Jonathan Edwards GBR	17.29m

WOMEN:

100m (-0.5):	Chryste Gaines USA	11.11
1500m:	Carla Sacramento POR	4:07.72
5000m:	Viktoria Nenasheva RUS	14:55.82
100mh (+0.6):	Lyudmila Engqvist SWE	12.67
JT:	Trine Hattestad NOR	65.48m

Nikaia Meeting
Nice, 10 July

MEN:

100m (-0.4):	Donovan Bailey CAN	10.17
1500m:	Hicham El Guerrouj MAR	3:30.61
2000m:	Noureddine Morceli ALG	4:49.55
3000m:	Paul Bitok KEN	7:32.05
400mh:	Torrance Zellner USA	48.24
HJ:	Charles Austin USA	2.34m
PV:	Igor Potapovich KZK	5.90m
HT:	Balazs Kiss HUN	81.76m

WOMEN:

100m (-1.4):	Mary Onyali NGR	11.18
400m:	Falilat Ogunkoya NGR	50.00
1500m:	Carla Sacramento POR	4:02.64
3000m:	Sonia O'Sullivan IRL	8:35.42
100mh (-0.4):	Lyudmila Engqvist SWE	12.67
JT:	Oksana Ovchinnikova RUS	65.10m

Securicor Games
London, 12 July

MEN:

100m (-1.7):	Michael Green JAM	10.26
400m:	Darnell Hall USA	44.68
1500m:	Venuste Niyongabo BUR	3:32.45
3000m:	Philip Mosima KEN	7:35.52
400mh:	Samuel Matete ZAM	48.40
HJ:	Charles Austin USA	2.31m
PV:	Maksim Tarasov &	
	Andrej Tiwontschik GER	5.85m
TJ:	Jonathan Edwards GBR	17.52m
SP:	Oliver Buder GER	19.91m

WOMEN:

100m (-0.2):	Juliet Cuthbert JAM	11.35
400m:	Cathy Freeman AUS	49.59
5000m:	Sonia O'Sullivan IRL	14:48.36
100mh (-1.7):	Michelle Freeman JAM	13.02
JT:	Tessa Sanderson GBR	64.06m

Herculis Vittel
Monte Carlo, 10 August

MEN:

100m (-0.2):	Donovan Bailey CAN	10.06

1500m:	Stephen Kipkorir KEN	3:32.17
3000m:	Daniel Komen KEN	7:25.16
400mh:	Samuel Matete ZAM	47.82
PV:	Maksim Tarasov RUS	5.80m
TJ:	Kenny Harrison USA	17.42m

WOMEN:

100m (+1.0):	Gwen Torrence USA	10.92
400m:	Marie-Jose Perec FRA	49.18
Mile:	Regina Jacobs USA	4:24.22
3000m:	Gabriela Szabo ROM	8:36.07
100mh (+0.6):	Michelle Freeman JAM	12.69
DT:	Ellina Zvereva BLR	64.96
JT:	Steffi Nerius GER	69.42m

Weltklasse
Zurich, 14 August

MEN:

100m (-1.4):	Dennis Mitchell USA	10.04
400m:	Anthuan Maybank USA	44.18
1500m:	Hicham El Guerrouj MAR	3:30.22
5000m:	Daniel Komen KEN	12:45.09
400mh:	Derrick Adkins USA	47.70
HJ:	Steinar Hoen NOR	2.28m
PV:	Igor Trandenkov RUS	5.95m
TJ:	Jonathan Edwards GBR	17.79m

WOMEN:

100m (-0.4):	Merlene Ottey JAM	10.95
Mile:	Svetlana Masterkova RUS	4:12.56 WR
100mh (-0.8):	Brigita Bukovec SLO	12.78
JT:	Steffi Nerius GER	68.80m

Weltklasse
Cologne, 16 August

MEN:

100m (+0.2):	Donovan Bailey CAN	10.03
1500m:	Hicham El Guerrouj MAR	3:33.45
3000m:	Khalid Boulami MAR	7:33.92
400mh:	Samuel Matete ZAM	48.02
PV:	Andrej Tiwontschik GER	5.95m

WOMEN:

100m (+0.2):	Merlene Ottey JAM	10.98
400m:	Marie-Jose Perec FRA	49.89
1500m:	Svetlana Masterkova RUS	4:04.54
5000m:	Gabriela Szabo ROM	14:44.42
100mh (+0.2):	Michelle Freeman JAM	12.85
LJ:	Inessa Kravets UKR	6.73m
JT:	Heli Rantanen FIN	67.82m

Memorial Ivo Van Damme
Brussels, 23 August

MEN:

100m (+0.4):	Dennis Mitchell USA	10.03
400m:	Michael Johnson USA	44.29
1500m:	Hicham El Guerrouj MAR	3:29.05
3000m:	Daniel Komen KEN	7:25.87
10,000m:	Salah Hissou MAR	26:38.08 WR
400mh:	Derrick Adkins USA	47.93
PV:	Tim Lobinger GER	5.85m
TJ:	Jonathan Edwards GBR	17.50m

WOMEN:

100m (-0.5):	Gail Devers USA	10.84
400m:	Cathy Freeman AUS	49.48
1000m:	Svetlana Masterkova RUS	2:28.98 WR
1500m:	Regina Jacobs USA	4:01.77
5000m:	Roberta Brunet ITA	14:58.96
100mh (+0.7):	Lyudmila Engqvist SWE	12.60
DT:	Ilke Wyludda GER	66.60m

ISTAF '96
Berlin, 30 August

MEN:

100m (-0.4):	Dennis Mitchell USA	10.08
Mile:	Noureddine Morceli ALG	3:49.09
5000m:	Daniel Komen KEN	13:02.62
400mh:	Torrance Zellner USA	48.23
PV:	Andrej Tiwontschik GER &	
	Igor Trandenkov RUS	5.86m
TJ:	Jonathan Edwards GBR	17.69m

WOMEN:

100m (-0.1):	Gail Devers USA	10.89
400m:	Falilat Ogunkoya NGR	50.31
1500m:	Svetlana Masterkova RUS	4:06.87
5000m:	Gabriela Szabo ROM	15:04.95
100mh (-0.2):	Michelle Freeman JAM	12.71
JT:	Tanja Damaske GER	66.60m

Grand Prix Final
Milan, 7 September

MEN:

100m (+1.5):	Dennis Mitchell USA	9.91
400m:	Michael Johnson USA	44.53
1500m:	Hicham El Guerrouj MAR	3:38.80
5000m:	Daniel Komen KEN	12:52.38
400mh:	Derrick Adkins USA	48.63
HJ:	Patrik Sjoberg SWE	2.33m
PV:	Maksim Tarasov RUS	5.90m
TJ:	Jonathan Edwards GBR	17.59m
SP:	John Godina USA	21.18m
HT:	Lance Deal USA	82.52m

WOMEN:

100m (+1.3):	Merlene Ottey JAM	10.74
400m:	Cathy Freeman AUS	49.60
1500m:	Svetlana Masterkova RUS	4:11.42
5000m:	Roberta Brunet ITA	14:54.54
100mh (+1.4):	Lyudmila Engqvist SWE	12.61
LJ:	Inessa Kravets UKR	7.07
DT:	Ilke Wyludda GER	64.74m
JT:	Tanja Damaske GER	66.28m

Grand Prix Final Standings

MEN:

Komen	103
Edwards	99
Mitchell	99
Morceli	93
Adkins	91
Matete	90
Bailey	85
Tarasov	79.5
Astapkovich	77
Kiss	77
El Guerrouj	77
Zellner	74

WOMEN:

Engqvist	93
Ottey	90
M Freeman	85
Ogunkoya	83
Kravets	80
Ovchinnikova	78
Wyludda	76
C Freeman	75
Damaske	72
Davis	71
Nerius	68
Torrence	66

6	April	Paris Marathon
13	**APRIL**	**FLORA LONDON MARATHON**
19–20	April	IAAF World Racewalking Cup, Prague
20	April	Rotterdam Marathon
21	April	Boston Marathon

4	May	IAAF Grand Prix, Rio
10	May	IAAF Grand Prix, Osaka
18	May	IAAF Grand Prix, Charlotte
		AAA V LOUGHBOROUGH STUDENTS, LOUGHBOROUGH
25	May	IAAF Grand Prix Prefontaine Classic, Eugue
25–26	**MAY**	**INTER COUNTIES, BEDFORD**
29	May	IAAF Grand Prix II, Seville
30	May	England v Latvia, Riga
31	May	IAAF Grand Prix II, San Jose
		IAAF Grand Prix II, Hengelo
		Michael Johnson v Donovan Bailey Challenge, Toronto
		WELSH GAMES, CARDIFF

2	June	IAAF Grand Prix II, St Denis
5	June	IAAF Grand Prix Golden Gala, Rome
7	June	Britain v Germany under-20, Mannheim
8	June	IAAF Grand Prix Znarnensky Memorial, Moscow
10	June	IAAF Grand Prix II, Bratislava
12–15	June	US World Championship trials, Indianapolis
13	June	England v Estonia, Tallin
14	**JUNE**	**BRITAIN V GERMANY V FRANCE UNDER-23, HEXHAM**
15	**JUNE**	**IAAF GRAND PRIX II, GATESHEAD**
18	June	IAAF Grand Prix II, Helsinki
21–22	June	European Cup Super League, Munich
21	June	England v Ireland, Cork
25	June	IAAF Grand Prix Gaz de France, Paris
28–29	**JUNE**	**NATIONAL VETS' CHAMPS, BLACKPOOL**
29	**JUNE**	**IAAF GRAND PRIX SECURICOR GAMES, SHEFFIELD**

2 July	IAAF Grand Prix Athletissima '97, Lausanne
4 July	IAAF Grand Prix Bislett Games, Oslo
5–6 JULY	**AAA UNDER-20 CHAMPIONSHIPS, BEDFORD**
7 July	IAAF Grand Prix DN Galan, Stockholm
9 July	IAAF Grand Prix II, Linz, Austria
10–13 July	European under-23 Cup, Turku, Finland
11–13 JULY	**TSB ENGLISH SCHOOLS CHAMPIONSHIPS, SHEFFIELD**
12–14 JULY	**GREAT BRITAIN WORLD CHAMPIONSHIPS TRIALS, BIRMINGHAM**
16 July	IAAF Grand Prix Nikaia, Nice
20 July	England v Ireland, Dublin
24–27 July	European Junior Championships, Ljubljana, Slovenia

1–10 August	IAAF World Championships, Athens
13 August	IAAF Grand Prix Weltklasse, Zurich
16 August	IAAF Grand Prix Herculis '97, Monte Carlo
18 AUGUST	**BUPA INTERNATIONAL CHALLENGE, CRYSTAL PALACE**
22 August	IAAF Grand Prix Ivo Van Damme, Brussels
24 August	IAAF Grand Prix Weltklasse, Cologne
26 August	IAAF Grand Prix ISTAF '97, Berlin
30 AUGUST	**GOLD CUP & JUBILEE CUP FINALS, BEDFORD**

3 September	IAAF Grand Prix II, Rieti
13 September	IAAF Grand Prix Final, Fukuoka, Japan
14 SEPTEMBER	**BUPA GREAT NORTH RUN, NEWCASTLE**
28 September	Berlin Marathon

| 4 October | IAAF World Half-Marathon Championships, Kosice, Slovakia |

| 2 November | New York City Marathon |

| 14 December | European Cross Country Championships, Oeiras, Portugal |

All fixtures are subject to alteration. Fixtures taking place in Britain in bold capitals.

Sport for Shelter

Are you attending sporting events throughout the year? Are you a runner, walker or maybe you fancy jumping out of a plane at 10,000 feet or bungee jumping? If so, why not consider raising money for Shelter at the same time?

Shelter is the largest, most established charity helping homeless and badly housed people and the only national one. Unique in the provision of practical help and advice as well as campaigning for long term change to tackle the problems of homelessness and poor housing.

Last year we helped over 100,000 people through our network of 50 Housing Aid Centres and projects countrywide whose caseworkers give free, impartial, professional legal and practical advice to those in housing need. Although rough sleeping is the most visible and severe form of homelessness many more households, including families with children, the elderly and vulnerable live in appalling conditions of squalor, overcrowding and insecurity; conditions which are totally unacceptable.

"I came to Shelter for help after I got into arrears following my husband's death. The building society wanted to repossess the house which has been my home for the last 25 years.

Shelter dealt with the building society, bank and solicitors. Shelter's help resulted in the building society agreeing to a monthly repayment I can afford and long term security. My family, and me especially, can't praise Shelter enough for all its done."

Shelter relies on the continued support of people like yourself to run its vital services. Total expenditure on the direct charitable objectives of housing aid services and communications in 1995/6 was £8.9 million and continues to rise with new projects and initiatives.

So run, walk, swim, jump.....for Shelter! Make a real difference to the lives of homeless and badly housed people around the country. For further information call 0171 505 2075.

Shelter

Registered Charity Number 263710
Registered Company Number 1038133

For the biggest names in sport, come to Sports Division.

(Or come second).

British Athletics Yearbook 1997

Free Prize Draw

TOP PRIZE

The **holiday of a lifetime** and a chance to support Britain's team in **Athens** at the sixth World Championships in Athletics.

Prize includes:

❶ Two return flights from London Heathrow to Athens

❷ 7 nights accommodation in a twin or double room at a four star hotel including breakfast

❸ Transfers between the airport and the hotel and vice versa

❹ Event tickets in the stadium for all full days that the winners are in Athens

❺ The services of WGT Travel Management's local representatives throughout their stay

SECOND PRIZE

£100 voucher for Olympus Sport + 2 tickets to either the BUPA World Trials [Incorporating the British Championships] 11-13 July 1997, Alexandra Stadium, Birmingham, or The GB v International Select 17 August, Crystal Palace, London.

THIRD PRIZE

2 tickets to either the BUPA World Trials or the GB v International Select + a years membership to the British Athletics Supporters Club.

No purchase necessary for a chance to win, fill in the form below and send to the listed address.
Rules: 1) Open to residents of the UK. 2) Proof of posting is not proof of receipt. No liability is accepted for applications lost. 3) The promoter's decision is final. 4) Closing date is 15/06/97. All claims must be received by this date. 5) For a list of major prize winners send a SSAE to the address below. 6) No cash alternatives to non-cash prizes. 7) Promoter - Kogan Page, 120 Pentonville Road, London N1 9JN. 8) Presentation of the prize may vary, however its value will remain the same. 9) Winners will be notified by telephone or post within a week of the closing date.

ENTRY FORM:

[Mr/Mrs/Ms/Miss]   First Name   ....

Surname   ....

Address   ....

....

....   Postcode   ....

Telephone   ....   Fax   ....

Signed   ....

Date   ....

KOGAN PAGE, 120 PENTONVILLE ROAD, LONDON N1 9JN

Index of Advertisers